CHAMPIONSHIP NO-LIMIT & POT-LIMIT HOLD'EM

"*Tom McEvoy and T. J. Cloutier [have] come up with the Bible on no-limit and pot-limit hold'em.*"
—Phil Helmuth, World Champion of Poker, 1989

"*T.J. Cloutier is head and shoulders above anyone else ... he is a legend ... the greatest living no-limit hold'em player in the world.*"
—Mansour Matloubi, World Champion of Poker, 1990

"*If there is one player that all of us fear the most at the final table, it is T. J. Cloutier.*"
—Berry Johnston, World Champion of Poker, 1986

"*Tom McEvoy's tournament advice is the best ever written.*"
—Barbara Enright, 1996 World Champion, Pot-Limit Hold'em

ABOUT THE AUTHORS

T. J. Cloutier won the Player of the Year award in 1998 and 2002, and is considered by most pros to be the best tournament player in the world. He has appeared at the championship table at the World Series of Poker a remarkable four times, placing second in 1985 and in 2000. Overall, he has won more titles in no-limit and pot-limit hold'em than any other tournament player in the history of poker. Cloutier, who has won four World Series of Poker bracelets, is the co-author of *Championship Omaha, Championship Tournament Practice Hands* and *Championship Hold'em.*

Tom McEvoy, the 1983 World Champion of Poker, has won four World Series titles. He is the author of the acclaimed *Championship Tournament Poker,* "one of the most important poker books of all time" according to Gamblers Book Club in Las Vegas. He is also the co-author of seven other titles: *Championship No-Limit & Pot-Limit Hold'em, Championship Stud, Championship Omaha, Championship Satellite Strategy, The Championship Table, Championship Tournament Practice Hands* and *Championship Hold'em.* McEvoy is also the author of "Tournament Talk," a gaming magazine column in which he advises players on correct tournament strategy.

CHAMPIONSHIP NO-LIMIT & POT-LIMIT HOLD'EM

T.J. CLOUTIER & TOM McEVOY

CARDOZA PUBLISHING

Cardoza Publishing is the foremost gaming and gambling publisher in the world with a library of more than 100 up-to-date and easy-to-read books and strategies. These authoritative works are written by the top experts in their fields and with more than 7,000,000 books in print, represent the best-selling and most popular gaming books anywhere.

FIRST CARDOZA EDITION

Copyright©1997, 2004 by T.J.Cloutier, Tom McEvoy & Dana Smith
- All Rights Reserved -

Library of Congress Catalog Card No: 2004100550
ISBN:1-58042-127-X

The authors can be emailed at:
   Tom   tommcevoy@cox.net
   T.J.   cardsmith@cox.net
Editorial consultant: Dana Smith
   Dana   pokerbooks@cox.net

Visit us at www.cardozapub.com or write to the address below for a full list of Cardoza books, advanced, and computer strategies.

CARDOZA PUBLISHING
P.O. Box 1500 Cooper Station, New York, NY 10276
Phone (800)577-WINS
email: cardozapub@aol.com
www.cardozapub.com

T.J. Cloutier (right) and Tom McEvoy, winner and runner-up at
Foxwoods Casino pot-limit hold'em tournament

T

TABLE OF CONTENTS

FOREWORD   **13**
by Mansour Matloubi, 1990 Champion, World Series of Poker

1. INTRODUCTION   **17**

2. GETTING TO KNOW YOUR OPPONENTS   **21**
OVERLY-AGGRESSIVE PLAYERS
    Keeping a Book
SETTING UP PLAYS
WATCHING THE QUALITY OF CARDS
OBSERVE THE OTHER PLAYERS
KNOW YOUR OWN HABITS
FOLLOW YOUR FIRST INSTINCT
PLAYER ANALYSIS

3. POT-LIMIT HOLD'EM STRATEGY   **37**
GOALS IN POT-LIMIT HOLD'EM
EFFECTS OF BLIND SIZE ON GAME STRATEGY
STARTING HANDS
    Big Pairs and Big Slick
    Ace-Small Suited
    Small Pairs
    Small Suited Connectors
    Two Big Cards
STARTING HANDS BY POSITION
RAISING HANDS
    When Not to Call a Raise
    The Purpose of the Pre-Flop Action

The Check-Raise
Playing the Blinds
PLAYING ON THE FLOP
Playing Second Pair in Late Position
Top Pair, Big Kicker
Walking Back to Houston
Playing Big Slick
Playing Draws
Playing Bottom Two Pair
Playing Big Pairs
Hitting a Set on the Flop
When You Flop an Overpair
Playing Pocket Aces
PLAYING ON THE TURN
Drawing Hands
The Bluff
The Big Bluff
Playing on the River

4. HOW TO WIN POT-LIMIT HOLD'EM TOURNAMENTS 89

TYPES OF PLAYERS
PERFECT TOURNAMENT STRATEGY
EARLY STAGE
Draws
The Maze
Middle Stage
Semi-Aggressiveness
Picking Your Spots
Playing a Short Stack
LATE STAGE
Betting Yourself Out of a Pot
THE LAST THREE TABLES
Playing a Big Stack
THE FINAL TABLE
Breaking Other Players
THE FINAL FIVE
Playing a Short Stack
PLAYING HEAD-UP
THE ZONE
"Move" Times in Tournaments
GETTING INTO THE MONEY

5. HOW TO WIN NO-LIMIT HOLD'EM TOURNAMENTS   115

NO-LIMIT HOLD'EM STYLE PLAYING STYLE
OBSERVATION
    Looking at Your Hand
TIMING IS EVERYTHING
MAKING MISTAKES
BUILDING AND PROTECTING YOUR CHIPS
TOURNAMENT STRUCTURE
TYPES OF HANDS TO START WITH IN EARLY POSITION
PLAYING THE SMALL PAIRS
PLAYING THE ACE-KING
THE RAISING HANDS FROM EARLY POSITION
THE STARTING HANDS IN MIDDLE POSITION
THE AMOUNT OF THE RAISE
    How Much Will They Call?
    Setting the Standard
    Varying the Size of Your Bets
BLUFFING
THE LUCK FACTOR
THE CLOCK
THE IMPORTANCE OF STACK SIZE
    Playing a Medium Stack
    Stack Size and Tournament Stage
    Playing a Short Stack
    Playing a Big Stack
    Moving Up the Ladder
PLAYING A PATIENT GAME
MATH AND POKER
THE NATURE OF NO-LIMIT POTS
PLAYING THE ACE-KING AFTER THE FLOP
    Against an Ace-Rag-Rag Flop
    When a Paint Comes on the Turn
    When the Flop Comes with Rags
BIG PAIRS AFTER THE FLOP
WHEN YOU FLOP A SET
    The Check Call and the Flat Call
THE RAISING HANDS AND THE RERAISING HANDS
PLAYING POCKET ACES
RERAISING WITH ACE-KING

PLAYING THE SMALL PAIRS
Small Pairs After the Flop
Jeopardy
SUITED CONNECTORS
A Rule for Suited Cards
PLAYING THE SMALL CONNECTORS
DANGER HANDS
PLAYING THE BLINDS
Picking Up the Blinds
Defending the Blind
GETTING TO THE FINAL TABLE
Sizing Up the Opposition
When You Get into the Money

6. HOW TO PRACTICE FOR WINNING THE WORLD SERIES OF POKER   181
GETTING EXPERIENCE
Small Tournaments
One-Table Satellites
Supersatellites
Your Best Value
SATELLITE STRATEGY
REBUY TOURNAMENTS
POST-TOURNAMENT STRESS
WORLD CLASS NO-LIMIT HOLD'EM PLAYERS

7. NO-LIMIT HOLD'EM PRACTICE HANDS   197
PRACTICE HAND 1
Scenario One • Scenario Two • Scenario Three
PRACTICE HAND 2
Scenario One • Scenario Two
PRACTICE HAND 3
Scenario One • Scenario Two
PRACTICE HAND 4
Scenario One • Scenario Two • Scenario Three
PRACTICE HAND 5
Scenario One • Scenario Two • Scenario Three
Scenario Four
PRACTICE HAND 6

Scenario One • Scenario Two
Flat Call on the Flop
Raise on the Flop
PRACTICE HAND 7
PRACTICE HAND 8
PRACTICE HAND 9
Scenario One • Scenario Two
PRACTICE HAND 10
PRACTICE HAND 11
Scenario One • Scenario Two
PRACTICE HAND 12
Scenario One • Scenario Two
PRACTICE HAND 13
The Scenario
PRACTICE HAND 14
Scenario One • Scenario Two • Scenario Three
PRACTICE HAND 15
An Example from the World Series
PRACTICE HAND 16
Analysis
PRACTICE HAND 17
Scenario One • Scenario Two • Scenario Three
PRACTICE HAND 18
Scenario One • Scenario Two
Ace-Small in Late Position
Ace-Small in the Blind
Ace-Middle Card
PRACTICE HAND 19
An Ace-Small Card Scenario in a
   Major No-Limit Hold'em Tournament
PRACTICE HAND 20
Another Ace-Small Card Scenario in a
   Big No-Limit Hold'em Tournament

8. TALES FROM T. J.   245
Jack "Tree Top" Straus and His Principle
George McGann, Robber-Player
Troy Inman, the "Protector"
A Very Unlucky Day in Odessa
Crawfish and Poker in Baton Rouge
The Poker Player with a Sense of Humor
Head-Up Against the Best
Little Red and Five-Card Stud

Where a Lot of Stories Begin and End
Kenny "Whatta Player" Smith
The Mystery Hand Play
The Worst Bad Beat of All Time
Speaking of Bad Beats ...
Mr. Brooks and the Two Jacks
The Best Woman Player in the World
The Worst Decision in the History of Poker
The Toughest Table in Tournament Poker

9. A CONVERSATION WITH T. J.   269
with Dana Smith

10. FINAL ADVICE   293

FOREWORD

BY MANSOUR MATLOUBI,
1990 CHAMPION,
WORLD SERIES OF POKER

T.J. Cloutier and Tom McEvoy have written a book that is very much needed by poker players. They may be giving too much away in *Championship No-Limit Hold'em and Pot-Limit Hold'em*, but that's okay with me! In fact, I was very surprised when T. J. told me that he and Tom were writing this book because in the past, there have been times at the poker table when I would say something to another player that I thought might help him, and T.J. would go ballistic about not wanting to "educate" the opposition. I am very glad that he has changed his mind.

All of the top poker players think that if they get lucky, they are unbeatable. But during the World Series of Poker, or in any other big no-limit tournament, if there is any player in the world that I would like to trade a piece with, it is T. J. Cloutier. When I first met him in 1989 in Malta, it was the first time that he had ever played against Europeans. After just a few hours of play, he basically knew everything about everybody who played poker in Europe. All he had to do was play you for a few hands and he knew exactly what you were made of and who was capable of doing what.

He sits in a tournament and moves from one table to

another table and he soon knows every poker player in the world; and if he doesn't, he will find out in a few minutes, quicker than anybody else that I know. Sometimes, I can't figure people out as quickly as he does, but the way that he plays them is a good enough example for me to follow. I have never seen anybody so strong.

We played head-up at the Diamond Jim Brady tournament in 1990 just after I had won the World Series of Poker. I was running good at the final table, making hands, betting and raising. But I never bluffed because, basically, I didn't need to. When the final hand came up, T.J. had a small pair and a flush draw, 7♥ 3♥. My hand was the 6♥ 9♥. Two overcards were on the board. There was no movement to this pot until the turn. A seven came on the turn, which gave T.J. a pair and gave me a straight draw. The river card was another overcard. He checked it and I bet all my chips. It was the first time at the final table that I had bluffed at the pot. With no hesitation, he called me with two sevens. No other player in the world would have done that! Later, we were joking about it.

This was the last $10,000 tournament at the Diamond Jim Brady; the first prize was $250,000 and second place was $160,000. There hadn't been a deal—we were playing for it all. How could this guy have read his opponent like that? I will never forget that hand, and I have told him many times that he made the greatest play that I have ever seen. He is the only player in the world that is capable of calling a pot like that. I think that T.J. is the best psychologist in the world!

Some of us might miss things at the poker table. We get involved in conversation and other things that are going on. But it seems to me that when T. J. is involved in conversation at the table, he still isn't missing a thing. Somehow, as he is talking, he is still playing his opponents correctly. It comes so naturally to him. I think the rest of us have to work hard at it. Sometimes, when we are making decisions about calling or not calling, we think about it for a few minutes and then might change our minds. But T.J.'s decisions are based on his first instinct. The first thing that crosses his mind is his last action. He acts more quickly than anyone else I know.

Tom McEvoy and I are more logical, mathematical and theoretical in our style. Basically, we are looking more at the value of the hand than the value of the opponent and that has been successful for us. T. J. would rather play his opponents than his cards. His emphasis is more on his opponents, picking his spots at the poker table, whereas Tom prefers to have the best hand. In this respect, I think that T. J. and Tom have the best partnership in writing this book. Tom writes the more theoretical part and T. J. does the more psychological aspects of the book.

I think that they are waking up the senses of people with the writing of this book. The first time that you read a book, it may not have an impact upon you. But over time, you become aware of the things that the authors are talking about. Probably, when T. J. was learning poker, there was no book to help him. But now, he and Tom are bringing their winning ideas to you. And in the end, this book will make a big difference.

T. J. has not won the World Series no-limit title yet, but in my opinion, he is the most deserving person to win it in the future. He is head and shoulders above anyone else. He is a legend. I believe that, by far, he is the number-one no-limit poker player in the world. ♠

T.J. and Tom feeling pretty good after another big win

INTRODUCTION

BY TOM MCEVOY
1983 CHAMPION, WORLD SERIES OF POKER

T. J. Cloutier and I first began talking about writing a poker book together several years ago, but we weren't sure exactly what type of book we should write. Between the two of us, we have won eight World Series of Poker titles and more than 100 other major titles in games ranging from razz to no-limit hold'em. In fact, T. J. holds more titles in pot-limit and no-limit hold'em than any other player in the world. After researching the books available on today's market, we decided that a manual that would help people learn how to win at no-limit and pot-limit hold'em would be the most valuable contribution that we could make. *Championship No-Limit and Pot-Limit Hold'em* is our way of giving something back to the world of poker, a world that has given both of us so much pleasure, excitement, and income over the past twenty-five years.

We also believe that this book will help to build the ranks of no-limit and pot-limit hold'em players. These are exciting poker games, games filled with intrigue, games that require an above average amount of skill. Some players are afraid to try playing them—they don't know how, or they may be afraid of the big-bet aspect of them, or maybe the "big" players that they think they will have to compete against in tournaments.

If you have been wanting to learn how to play no-limit or pot-limit hold'em but have been reluctant to try playing them for any of these reasons, throw your reservations out the window and dig into *Championship No-Limit and Pot-Limit Hold'em*—we wrote this book for you.

We don't use any fancy language and we leave no gaps in explaining how you can win. Our editor, Dana Smith, tells me that we aren't boring, either. T. J. discusses how to play no-limit and pot-limit in the same way that he talks—in that good ol' Texas poker player lingo that everybody who has ever heard him speak agrees is colorful, and simple, and brilliant. He even allows me to make an occasional comment about the play of a hand. In fact we have made it a point to give you our different views on strategy because we think that you deserve to know that not everybody agrees on exactly how to play poker.

We also include plenty of hand illustrations to let you see what you are reading, to visualize yourself in a particular scenario, and to analyze how you would play in different situations. T. J. tells you how hands have been played in actual games at the World Series of Poker, in Texas, and in California. I don't think he's ever forgotten a hand he's played or a face he has seen or the playing style of anybody he has played against. His memory is incredible and his talent is awesome.

What we have tried to do in this book is to bring you T.J.'s vast reservoir of experience and expertise in games that he learned as a road gambler in Texas. He is a seasoned veteran who has earned his stripes on battle fields ranging from dingy backroom games to the glitz and glamour of the World Series of Poker. I am proud to be a friend of T. J.'s and I am proud of this book that we have created together.

As soon as you have tried some of the strategies that we suggest, write me a note. Let me know your reactions to our book and the results that you are getting, and I'll send you a personal thank you. With the knowledge that you have learned from *Championship No-Limit & Pot-Limit Hold'em*, and a little bit of experience under your belt, I am confident that we will meet one day soon in the winners' circle. ♠

2

GETTING TO KNOW YOUR OPPONENTS

THE MOST VALUABLE SKILL IN BIG-BET POKER

It has always been my belief that knowing your opponents in pot-limit and no-limit hold'em—how they usually play, and how they play in specific situations—is the most important thing in the game. I once took a friend who didn't play much poker to a game with me. He saw us talking when we were out of a hand, and then he noticed me talking to a guy across the table while a hand was being played. He asked me, "How can you tell what's going on if you're talking? How do you know what your opponents are doing?"

"If a wing fell off a gnat at the end of the table, I'd see it," I told him. What I was trying to get across to him was that you have to be alert at all times. When you're not in a hand, you can learn something very valuable. If you're going to be successful at pot-limit or no-limit hold'em, you've gotta' be able to sit down at a table with eight or nine people that you've never played with in your life, and after ten or fifteen minutes, know how each one of them plays—whether they're aggressive; whether they're passive; how they play early position, middle position, late position. You have to get an initial line on their play.

We're just like leopards: We can't change our spots. A fella' who used to play with us in Texas years ago would play as good a poker game as anybody I'd ever seen play— for the first two hours. You could've put a stop watch on him. He'd hit a stone wall after two hours and then his whole game would revert back to the way he always played. He would start bluffing in bad spots, and started giving his money away. With a player like that, you can just wait on him. You know he's going to crumble in two hours, so wait him out. You're going to win the money.

I might forget a person's name, but I'll never forget his face or how he plays in all situations, no matter if I've only played with him one time in my life. The main thing is being very observant and watching what players do in different situations. If a player has raised before the flop with A-K and the flop comes with three babies, is he the type of player who will lead with this hand? Or is he the type of player who will check his A-K because he doesn't have anything yet? Suppose somebody else bets when the baby flop hits, and he calls. What does that tell you?

It tells me that he has committed a mortal sin in poker. If you don't flop to it, get rid of your hand. But you see pot-limit and no-limit players who call in this situation all the time, especially when you're playing against people who are used to playing limit hold'em. They're going to bet A-K against a board with three babies, or they're going to call with A-K. But you always have an edge on them if you know how they play in that spot.

OVERLY-AGGRESSIVE PLAYERS

Then there are players who are overly aggressive. If you watch them very carefully, you will find that they can't stand two checks. So, you check to them twice—you have a big hand and you check to them *twice*. Let them eat themselves up. Even some of the legendary players who have had a lot of success on the circuit can't stand two checks and you can trap some of these big-name players by just checking it to them two times. Some of the really aggressive players such as Stu Ungar fit into this category.

In tournament poker, you can come over the top of these aggressive players. You know their level of tolerance, that they can't stand two checks. You don't even need a hand to win the pot! All you need to do is play back against them on fourth street. When you're running good, they'll throw their hands away every time. And then the one time that you really have a hand and make this play, that's the time when they'll call you. Timing is everything in poker.

One of the main concepts in pot-limit and no-limit is that there are situations when you don't need to have a hand to win a good pot, whereas in limit hold'em, you have to show down a hand almost every time.

KEEPING A BOOK

I have almost a photographic memory about situations in poker, so I don't need to go home and write things down, but I think that it's a good practice for most players. After your session, go home and think about the game and the players. During an eight-hour session, thirty to forty key hands will be played. You should be able to remember these hands. Keep a little book on all the players, what they did in these key hands, because they're going to do the same thing the next time you play them. And you're going to be the recipient of their generosity, of their playing patterns.

For example, I know a player who will always bring it in for a small raise when everybody has passed to him on the button; he never comes in flat. And he's a good enough player that he doesn't stand a reraise unless he has a big hand. Knowing that he plays very aggressively off the button, you can make a lot of money from this man when you're in the little blind or the big blind by just popping him back three or four times in a session. Obviously, if you do it every time, you're going to get yourself killed, but you can tell when to do it.

The thing that I've always thought about hold'em is that if you're playing nine-handed and six players have passed to you on the button, there's a pretty good chance, with eighteen cards already dealt out, that somebody behind you might have a hand since nobody in front of you does. Tom calls that "the bunching factor." In *Championship Tournament Poker*, he mentions that it doesn't necessarily have to work that way, but it seems reasonable to assume that if everybody has passed, it is more likely than usual that the blinds, or possibly the button, could have a legitimate hand.

Remember that when you're on the button, you're in the power position. The blinds will always have to act before you do after the flop. A lot of times, you don't have to make that button raise. If you just call, they will have to come to you. And when they have to come to you, that gives you all the options in the world after you've seen the flop. Contrary to what a lot of players do, I limp on the button quite often, unless I have a big hand. Many players in tournaments get into the habit of raising on the button with no hand to pick up the blinds. Sometimes, I might steal a guy's button by making that play from just in front of the button—I'm not always on the button when I try to steal.

In a tournament I recently played, a player had raised on the button against my big blind about ten straight times. Three times, I had gone over the top of him. In this particular hand, he came in for a small raise when I had A-J in the big blind. I knew that this man was going to make a move on me, he's that type of player. I had played with him before and remembered how he played. So I raised him. Then he says, "I'm moving all in." All I had was A-J, but I knew that I had the best hand. And sure enough, I did have the best hand: He had 9-6 offsuit. He got lucky and won the pot when he flopped two nines, but that's not the point. The play was correct in the way that I had set it up.

SETTING UP PLAYS

Pot-limit and no-limit hold'em are games in which you can set up plays. At Vegas World years ago, I was watching "Joe Dokes" play. Since then, Joe has turned into a very decent player and has finished high in a lot of tournaments, but this incident happened when he first started on the poker scene. It was passed to me on the button and I made a play at the pot with A-7 offsuit because the blinds were pretty good sized. Joe reraised me from the big blind. I had more chips than he had, and I knew that there was only one hand that he could have that he would call me with if I moved in on him over the top for the third raise. He would have to have aces. Seeing that I had an ace, I made the play and went all-in on him. Joe had two kings, but he threw them away. Then I showed him the A-7. For a purpose.

About thirty-five minutes later, I had two sevens on the button. It was passed to me and I made a slight raise. Joe called and I knew that he was trying to trap me by the way that he acted when he called. He screwed up to the table and made a few moves that I had observed before. The flop came 7-4-2. He checked to me, I bet, and he beat me to the pot moving in. He had a big pair and I ate him alive with the trip sevens. Joe got trapped because of the A-7 that I had showed him previously. You see, one play can set up another play, and you have to think this way all the time that you're playing.

Of course, these types of plays are far more common in pot-limit and no-limit than they are in limit hold'em. I think that limit hold'em is a game that you have to play so much tighter than you play pot-limit and no-limit. You don't have many different moves. Tom describes limit hold'em as being much more technical, a game where you have to show down some hands.

Several good players that I know raise with some funny hands. For example, Phil Hellmuth raises with some hands that I would never consider raising. And he calls with hands that I wouldn't call with. People looking on will say, "How could he make that play? And he wins with it!" But he has a reason for doing it. It all depends on who he's playing with and what he's trying to accomplish. When you get to the top rung of the ladder, the skill level is extremely high. You can set up players in no-limit, but you can't set them up very often in limit. McEvoy says that it's so easy for them to call in limit poker that it limits your options.

Don't ever be a calling station in pot-limit or no-limit. But when you do call, make sure that you have a good purpose. Of course, there are some times when you do call. Say the flop comes 9-8-7. You have Q-J in your hand, you have a lot of chips in front of you, and so does your opponent. He makes a decent bet on the flop. There's nothing wrong with calling one time because you have two overcards and a straight draw. If you pop that ten to make your straight on the turn, you now have the nuts, and can play the hand many different ways in order to win a pretty good-sized pot. In limit hold'em, you expect to see this play, but in no-limit, you don't expect it. It's not something that you'd ever try to do with a short stack in a tournament either; it depends on your stack size against him, and your pot odds.

WATCHING THE QUALITY OF CARDS

You have to watch the quality of cards that you play, and the quality of cards that your opponents play. Limit players play big cards—K-Q, Q-J, J-10, K-J, K-10, suited or unsuited—that's the nature of the game. *In no-limit, these are absolute trap hands.* If you flop top pair with any of those hands, there is a very good chance that you'll wind up with second-best hand and get broke to it. You don't stand raises with hands like 10-8 or J-8 in a tournament at a full table. You'll get trapped with any of these hands.

So, you keep a book on everybody and you put in it the kinds of hands they play. McEvoy and I started playing together around 1979, and I'm sure that he knows what I do, and I know what he does, too. We've watched all the really good players over the years—and every one of them has a tell. Even legendary players like Phil Hellmuth, John Bonetti, Stu Ungar, Doyle Brunson. If you observe enough and watch them play hands for long enough, you'll find that they all have a certain tell when they have a really *big* hand versus just a hand. Of course, the top players don't show tells very often, but they *do* do it. And that's pretty true of everybody else in poker, too.

For example, one top-notch tournament player has a way of betting his chips. He starts to make a call and then goes back to get more chips and says, "Raise." Every time this player makes that go-back move, he's there with a hand. Another player has a "hitch" move when he has a big hand. He'll come out with the amount that he's supposed to call with, hesitate out there with his hand, go back to his stack, and then come back out with a raise. Every time he does this, he's got a big hand. If he doesn't do it, there's a bigger chance that he has a mediocre hand. In other words, if his move is more fluid, he usually doesn't have quite the strength that he is representing.

These are fabulous things to know about your opponents. And you get to know them only through observation.

OBSERVE THE OTHER PLAYERS

Observe all of the players as the cards are being dealt. As people are making bets, always look at the people in front of and behind you. I look at my cards when I first get them so that I can observe the board; I don't wait for the action to get to me before I look at my hand. If you're looking at your hand when the action gets to you, rather than looking at the people behind you that haven't acted yet, you're missing a lot. It's the old "load-up" theory. There are a lot of poker players who can't stand it when they pick up a big hand, and so they'll load up their hands with chips before it's their turn. If you're observant, you'll throw down a mediocre hand because you know that the guy behind you is going to raise. It happens many, many times.

KNOW YOUR OWN HABITS

One time when I was just starting out in poker, I caught myself in the habit of pushing my cards back into my chips whenever I had a big hand, instead of just leaving them out there. "Well," I thought after I had discovered my own tell, "maybe I can use this in reverse." So, one or two times during a game, I'd push my cards back toward my chips when I didn't have a hand. And boy, it worked!

You have to know your own characteristics. How many times have you had the absolute nuts, and you have an opponent who is a pretty loose player, and you want him to call you? And he starts icing you down, looking at you before he calls to see whether you have a tell or are giving any clues. At those times, I've swallowed hard and looked to the side, trying to induce him to call. So, you can use some of these tells in *reverse* to your favor.

FOLLOW YOUR FIRST INSTINCT

Tom told me a story about second-guessing himself on a player's tell.

"I was in there with a pretty weak hand, an A-5, which I had raised with from a middle position before the flop. I'd been catching some hands and my table image was strong. Freddy Deeb called my raise. The flop came J-J-5. I bet the flop and Deeb called. A nothing-card came off on the turn and I checked. So did he. Another blank came on the river and I checked again. Then Freddy made a big bet at the pot. I looked at him and his hand was trembling. My first instinct was to muck my hand, but I thought that he looked awfully nervous and might be putting a play on me. I called and he turned up a J-6 suited. So, detecting nervousness doesn't necessarily mean weakness; it could mean strength, too. As it turns out, he was nervous that I might *not* call him!"

I have an opinion on those types of hands. When it comes J-J-5 like that, if you have raised going in and the man stood the raise, you don't have anything. He could have two sixes in the hole and have you beat. Once you make your little cursory bet at this pot, you're through with this hand if you get called. You're completely through with it: You cannot lose any more money to this hand, I don't care *what* the opponent has. Tom admits that his gut instinct was, "Okay, I'm done with it." But trying to pick off the tell, he second-guessed himself.

Your first instincts are better than 95 percent correct

if you're a poker player. That's because your first instinct comes from all the training and practice and skills that you've learned over the years. What you think *after* your first instinct is the type of thinking that goes, "What hands can I beat?" You *never* think about what hands you can beat. "Do I have the best hand?" is what you should be thinking.

Remember, a bettor be, a caller never. If you're calling in a poker game, you're calling because you've set a man up and you want him to bet you. You have two chances at the pot by betting: Either he'll muck his hand, or you have the best hand. When you're calling, your chances are slim and none unless you've set things up for a call.

My wife Joy was sitting on the sidelines watching us play at Binion's in 1994 when I won the pot-limit hold'em tournament at the World Series. She heard the people around her saying, "What's happening? T.J.'s not playing any pots. He's got chips, but he's just sitting there." A fella who had watched me play a lot of tournaments said, "You watch what happens when they get down to three players. The money's in the top three positions. Just watch him open up and get aggressive *then*."

And that's exactly what happened. When you're playing tournament poker, the money's in the top three spots and you've got to get there. Sure, you're going to play marginal hands sometimes, and you're going to play different situations. But you cannot do that all of the time. You have to use correct timing.

PLAYER ANALYSIS

Now let's analyze the play of a top-notch tournament player who has won some major titles. I'm going to call him "John Smith." Smith has a very big "sizz" potential. When players like Smith get a very big hand beaten, what do they do during the next ten or fifteen minutes? That's when you look for the potential sizz, the tilt factor.

A lot of players become overly aggressive when they take a bad beat. They will play a hand that they shouldn't be in with, get a little flop to it, and then get it beat—and then they get even crazier. Smith often does this when he gets a hold of a lot of chips. He's a truly great player, but he has a bad habit of thinking that nobody else at the table can play. So, he thinks that because he makes a move at the pot, his opponents should automatically lose the pot to him. But it doesn't happen that way. Any player should be able to take any kind of a beat and not let it change his style one iota. Over 10,000 or 100,000 hands, everybody is going to catch the same kinds of cards. It's how you play them that comes out in the wash.

When Smith breaks his chips down to call, he will turn them out in stacks of five or so, then he'll stack them up, and then he'll go back to the stack, then bring them back out and stack them up again. And he usually makes the call or a raise when he does this. When he goes back and forth with his chips, most of the time he has a big hand. And he usually cuts off his chips to the right. But every once in a while, I've seen him cut them off to the left. Now, when he stacks them reverse to his usual pattern, he's usually on a draw or a bluff. This is just an example of the things that you can observe in a poker game and use to your advantage.

You can expect Smith to play very good poker unless he takes a very bad beat. Then he sizzles. So, the time to get a jump on a player like Smith is during the ten or fifteen minutes after he takes a bad beat. You're going to take beats in poker, that's all there is to it. Just watch out for the sizz.

Then there's the type of player who splashes his chips in front of him—he never stacks his chips in front of him, he just splashes them out toward the pot. Suppose he's been doing this all day long in your game. Then suddenly, he cuts his chips out and stacks them up very nicely. Now that's a big difference in his usual style. When he splashes his chips, does he have a hand or doesn't he have a hand, as opposed to what he has when he stacks them out neatly? If you've been watching him, you'll know. Now you've learned something about this player—which way he has a hand, and which way he doesn't have one, or whether the way he puts in his chips means anything at all. It may not, but usually it does.

Like I said before, people always revert back to their own styles.Tom points out that a lot of players in a tournament play their A-games for an hour or so, until they can't stand it any longer. Then they all go back to their natural style of play. Maybe they've been trying to play real snug or real solid, whatever they think their A-game is. Some of the better players may even hold out for two hours. Of course, Tom's not talking about the great players who get the money most of the time in tournaments.

There are a lot of players in tournaments who don't have an A-game. These players can be very dangerous because anybody can pick up two cards and get a flop to them. But in the long run, the weaker players are going to make calls and plays that are so far out of line that they don't have a chance to win the tournament.

Every now and then, somebody will come along like the late Hal Fowler. It might have been the biggest upset in the history of poker when he won the World Series in 1979. He made four or five inside straights at the final table—three of them against Bobby Hoff when they were playing head-up. You could've played as good as God can play, and you couldn't have won those pots. You can't win a tournament when a man is doing that to you for a big amount of money.

But regardless of these types of amazing things that occasionally happen, still play your A-game and maintain your observation powers. Observation is such a strong tool, and knowing how the other people play in various situations with different hands, and keeping that book on everybody are so important that I can't say it often enough. Observation is the strongest thing in pot-limit and no-limit poker.

T.J. wins again!

3

POT-LIMIT HOLD'EM STRATEGY

Pot-limit hold'em is the next jump up from limit hold'em. You can bet what is in the pot at any time, but *only* what is in the pot at any time. In my opinion, pot-limit hold'em is a great game when it is played with a high blind structure. No-limit is a great game with any blind structure. The main difference between the two games is that in pot-limit, because of the size of the bets that you are forced to make, you cannot run people out of the pot with a big bet like you can do in no-limit. In no-limit, you can protect your hand (if you want to) by putting in a big raise. No-limit hold'em is an aggressive game. Pot-limit is a semi-aggressive game.

You cannot protect big pairs before the flop in pot-limit unless you limp in, and somebody raises, and there's a reraise, and then you raise again so as to get some people out of the pot with a big raise. You have more opportunities for trap plays in pot-limit. And in pot-limit, you can raise with some hands that you can't raise with in no-limit. But after that, your aggression should shut down a little bit. There are a lot of players taking shots with the same hands in pot-limit and you can get yourself in a trap, whereas in no-limit, you can bet enough money to put people to a test every time.

There are two ways of playing pot-limit hold'em. In straight pot-limit, if there is a $5 and a $10 blind, you can call the $10 and raise $25. The second player can call the size of the pot, or raise the size of the pot with his bet in it. The second game structure uses the old formula that used to be used a lot in pot-limit games, in which the opening bet can be four times the size of the big blind. Another way that we used to play in Texas was to round off the bets to the nearest $25. Instead of having to figure out a lot of little bets, we would simply round it up. If there was $180 in the pot, we could bet up to $200.

But the main feature about pot-limit hold'em is the protection procedure. It is a game designed for people who will take flops to hands like 4-5, 5-6, or 7-8 suited for a minimum amount of money. If a player brings it in for $40 and you can play for just $40, you might be able to take someone off who has a big hand. If an opponent has two aces or two kings, for example, and the flop comes out 3-6-7, he's not going to give you credit for 4-5, he's coming out betting. So, a lot of times, you can trap a player in pot-limit. You can't do it as much in no-limit because it costs you too much to make that call.

Because of this, a lot of people prefer pot-limit to no-limit hold'em. Pot-limit is a game that gives players a chance to play a lot of little pairs; it is designed for that. Some players who are very aggressive will put in a lot of small raises, hoping to flop something. For a minimum bet, the size of the big blind in an unraised pot, or four times the big blind if someone brings it in for that amount, you can play pocket sixes or sevens—and you might flop something. It is a game that is completely different from no-limit in this respect.

In addition to the small pairs, some players will even try to sweeten the pot with a little pot-builder raise with hands like J-10 or 9-8 suited. They're hoping to build a pot with their modest raises to make sure that there's a little something in the pot in case they hit a hand. There's nothing wrong with this strategy *if* you're a good enough player to get away from a hand.

Say that you raise with:

You get two or three callers. Then the flop comes:

Now, how do you play the hand? That's the big question. If you bet and get any action on the hand, there's a pretty good chance that you're beaten already. So, you have to be skilled enough to know when your hand is good and when it isn't. And that goes back to the first chapter on observation and knowing how other people play.

There are many times when you will check this hand (in the example above) because you want to find out where you are. Any time that you hear somebody say, "I made a bet to find out where I was," you know that person is making a bad play, because it is foolish to put money into a pot to find out where you are. You should be observant enough and play well enough to find that out without having to put money in the pot.

I've heard so many players say that they've bet $200 at a pot because they "wanted to see where I was." To me, that is a ridiculous statement in poker. Why would you *ever* do something like that?

Suppose you put in $200 and some guy raises you. What are you going to do with the hand? You're going to throw it away. But if you had checked and the man then made a decent bet, you would know that he had some kind of hand. Then it's up to you whether you want to call him. You sure wouldn't have wasted that $200!

GOALS IN POT-LIMIT HOLD'EM

The main idea that drives a good pot-limit player's actions is maximizing the amount of money that he can win on a hand. A good pot-limit player can maximize the money that he can win because his betting sequences are correct. If you have a hand that you can raise with, you want to build the pot, *not* limit the field.

I don't believe in varying the size of your bets, either. I always bet the size of the pot. If you always bet the size of the pot, your opponents can't get a tell on you, or a tell on what kind of a hand you have. So many players give away information by the size of their bets. A big-time player that I know has the biggest tell in the world: When he makes a baby raise, he has a big hand, and when he makes a big raise, he has a marginal hand. This reverse tell of his is as pure as the driven snow. He's always afraid that he won't get called if he puts in a big raise when he has a big hand.

Once again, you can learn this type of information about players if you are always observing their play and keeping a mental or written book on them. In pot-limit, when you have the chips and you have the hand that you want to play, you won't be giving away any information if you always bet the size of the pot.

EFFECTS OF BLIND SIZE ON GAME STRATEGY

Does the size of the game affect the way that you play? My theory is that it does not. Say that you have your choice of three pot-limit games: a $5-$10, a $10-$10, and a $10-$25. To play the $10-$25 game, you should have enough bankroll to play. Even if your bankroll is four or five times the amount you need to play the game, you're still going to play it the same way. You should play the same hands, no matter what the structure. In side games, your strategy should not be affected by the size of the blinds.

Personally, I like to play in games with a high blind structure because then I can get more protection for my hands. You should have the same standards for the hands that you play regardless of the size of game you're playing. Some people will play looser when they're playing in cheaper games, play hands that aren't as good as they would play in higher limit games, because they figure that it isn't costing them much to play. They are the losers. If your standards are the same for every size of game you play, you're going to get the money.

A good player doesn't hope to get a 60-40 break in the cards. If the cards break even, a good player will win the money—at all times—because he's going to make fewer mistakes than a bad player will make. What does poker break down to in the long run? Most of the money you make comes from somebody's mistakes. Good players also make mistakes, but they make fewer of them.

In tournament play, though, the size of the blinds does affect your play. As you progress in a tournament, you will have more chips (or you won't progress). As the blinds increase, your chips should increase. Of course, the rise in blinds shouldn't affect your play a lot, but you do have to be a little bit more selective on your starting hands. Hold'em is a position game, and you're going to play your position strong as the levels go up, no matter what the blinds are.

STARTING HANDS

We all know the standard hands to start with in hold'em, and we know that big pairs are the strongest starting hands. But when some people begin to rate starting hands, they will rank them in this order: two aces, two kings, A-K, two queens. They put A-K before two queens. I don't.

BIG PAIRS AND BIG SLICK

I rate the big-card starting hands as aces, kings, queens, jacks, tens, and *then* A-K. I realize that some computer people rank A-K higher, but if you play day-to-day, you'll see the value in ranking Big Slick below the high pairs. Tom rates A-K below queens, on about the same par as jacks, so we're fairly close in our thinking.

The reason that I go all the way down to tens before throwing in Big Slick is because you can still make the nut straight with a 10. (You cannot make a straight in hold'em without a ten or a five.) Plus, you will make more nut straights (ace-high) with a ten than with any other card. With tens, you can make the A-K-Q-J-10 straight, all the way down to the 10-9-8-7-6 straight—and those hands do come up. That is why I rate a pair of tens above A-K as a starting hand.

ACE-SMALL SUITED

I have been asked if there is a time when you would play Ace-small suited in pot-limit. Sure there is, because you can get in so cheaply in an unraised pot. That's one of the main ideas in pot-limit hold'em. If you can get in for a cheap price, why not take a flop to Ace-small suited? You can come into an unraised pot from any position with the hand, and then if someone raises behind you, you can always throw it away and it hasn't cost you much.

Remember that when you are playing Ace-small (A-2, A-3, A-4, A-5), there are a number of hands that you can either flop or make, including a nut flush, a straight, two pair, and sometimes even a small set such as three deuces, treys, fours, or fives—and all of these sets have the top kicker, the ace, to go with them.

SMALL PAIRS

You also can start with small pairs, depending on the size of the pair, your position, and the action. You might play hands like deuces, treys, fours, or fives, from fifth position or later. Suppose that you're in fifth or sixth position in a $10-$10 game, a player has brought it in for a small raise of $40, and there already are three players in the pot. The pot is laying you good odds, so why not call the $40 with your small pocket pair? If you flop a set, you're probably going to win a good-sized pot. If you don't flop a set, you can get away from it and all it has cost you is your original bet.

It is the weak players who trap themselves with the small pairs. Say that the flop comes J-8-6 and a player bets on the flop. The weak player is holding a pair of fours and he calls, hoping to catch a four on the turn. That is a horrible play. For the number of times that you will catch your card in that instance, you might lose thirty times. And even if you do catch it, you might be up against a larger set and end up losing your whole bankroll. Calling with an underpair on the flop is limit strategy, and limit strategy doesn't work in pot-limit hold'em. Tom and I both agree that even in limit hold'em, it is a bad play to call with an underpair on the flop. But if you play regularly, you will see players doing it thousands of times.

Tom notes that "If I'm in a rammer-jammer game where there's a lot of pre-flop raising, the small pairs and suited connectors don't play very well because it gets to be too expensive to see the flop with them. But when you're in a normal pot-limit game where there's a lot of limping going on and just an average amount of raising, you can limp in with the small pairs out of position, even from an early position in pot-limit hold'em.

"I will call a small raise if it looks like I'm going to get multiway action on my small pair. For example, if a couple of people have limped and then a player raises the pot to $40 or $50, the gamble is worth it because the im-

CLOUTIER & MCEVOY • CARDOZA PUBLISHING

plied odds are there. Sometimes, your call of a small raise will attract other callers and then you are almost guaranteed to get a good price on your hand. So what if you miss the flop? You're only in there for a small amount and you have the chance to win a big pot."

I disagree somewhat with Tom on the way that he plays the small pairs. I believe that when you compare the number of times that you will flop a hand with your small pair and get a play on the hand after the flop, with the number of times that you will burn up $40 or $50 making the call, the numbers don't even out. In the long run, I think that you will be a loser to the small pairs. First of all, if you catch a set to the small pair, you have to get a play on the flop. You might go twenty or thirty hands without hitting a flop. Unless you have a big cash reserve in a pot-limit ring game, you can run through a lot of money that way.

Of course, Tom is talking about the times that he calls a raise with small pairs when it looks like the pot is going to develop multiway, whereas I am discussing opening with small pairs from an early position. If it looks like he's going to be playing head-up, then Tom doesn't call the raise. He only calls it if it looks like the pot is going to be played multiway.

SMALL SUITED CONNECTORS

Pot-limit is designed for playing suited connectors for the same reason that it is designed for playing a small pair: You can get in cheaply with the connectors.

Say that you are on the button with the following:

45

The pot has been raised, three or four people have called the pot, and it costs you $40 to call. You can take a flop to this type of hand for $40. You might flop the nuts and break somebody who is holding a big overpair. If you don't flop to it, it's the easiest hand in the world to get away from.

It's a different scenario in no-limit. Seeing a flop with these types of hands in no-limit probably will cost you a lot of money, but in pot-limit side games, you can take flops with them. With the small connectors, you might flop two pair, three-of-a-kind, or a straight, all of which can be good hands. If you watch a great player like Bobby Hoff playing in side games, you'll notice that he seldom wins with hands like aces, kings, or queens. When he's on the button with two connectors, he'll bring it in for a baby raise every single time. The cards don't even need to be suited.

If you look at computer runs, they will tell you that suited connectors are always better than nonsuited connectors. But the computer doesn't factor into the equation that there may be three or four other players in the pot who could be holding cards in your same suit—and there's a good chance of that happening.

My thinking in pot-limit is that when you play connectors, they don't necessarily need to be suited because when they are suited, they can become trap hands. There is more value in the cards being *connected* than in being suited. In fact, a lot of times, you don't want to be suited with those small connectors because if the flop comes two-to-a-suit, there's a chance that you might be up against a higher flush draw, and then the hand can cost you a lot of money.

Tom doesn't favor suited connectors as much in the early positions because you usually have to make a lot of tricky judgment plays. Sometimes, you'll make something with your hand and still have to muck it, especially when you flop a flush draw. Other times, you'll flop top pair with a straight draw, but you're out of position — and then what do you do?

The broke player's lament as he's walking out the door from a pot-limit or no-limit game is "I lost a big pot calling with a such-and-such hand ... but I was suited." Big deal! There are a lot of times when your suit comes up, but there are also a lot of times when it doesn't. Of course, if you have A♥ K♥ against A-K offsuit, you're a favorite. You're a *slight* favorite, but still you are a favorite for the few times that the flop comes in your suit. I've also seen two aces against two aces, four-of-a-suit comes, and one of the players wins the pot with his suited ace. When that happens, it's like the rub of the green in golf or just being unlucky in poker.

When you're in a head-up situation in a raised pot, you cannot call with the connectors. The pot has to be laying you odds for you to play them — three or four players in the pot. You don't want to be head-up with a drawing hand where you have to get lucky to flop to it. When you're head-up, you want to have a hammer.

You don't want to play the small suited connectors in

tournaments, either, because you can't reach into your pocket for more chips. In tournaments, I don't play the connectors because I always try to play top hand if I can.

TWO BIG CARDS

Many players will play any two big cards from any position, but that is not a good idea, in my opinion. Let's start with A-J, the biggest trash hand that you can play, and also the biggest trap hand of the trash hands. Take a look at this scenario. You are holding:

Say that you're in a pot for a little raise, or maybe you're playing in an unraised pot with three or four players. The flop comes:

You can get trapped very easily with A-J. You might be against A-K, A-Q, any two pair, or any set. From an early position in side games, A-J is a good hand to dump. K-J, K-Q, K-10 — all of these types of hands — are dangerous. If you don't flop a straight to them, or flop a full house to them (when you flop two of one rank and one of the other rank), you're in trouble.

What do you want to catch to these types of hands?

You don't want to make top pair because chances are that you'll be outkicked, or somebody might hold an overpair. I like the small and medium connectors better than two big cards. Of course, if it's passed to you on the button when the only hands to act after you are the blinds, then these hands might have some value. But in early positions, they are horrible hands.

When can you play two big cards in pot-limit hold'em? I prefer having the action passed to me when I'm in one of the back four positions. Then, I will play hands that I normally wouldn't play, hands such as K-Q, K-J, or K-10, for example. When you call with two big cards from a late position, there is a fairly good chance that you won't get raised, and even if you do, you have only called the original bet and the hand is easy to get away from.

Suppose that you flat called before the flop with:

Only the two blinds and you are in the pot. The flop comes:

If one of the two blinds leads at the pot, you probably would just flat call; but if they both check, then you would bet. The reason that you would flat call the blind's bet in an unraised pot is because he could have any two random cards and could have flopped two pair.

Random cards get a lot of people in trouble. You can get into trouble by betting bottom two pair or a king with a weak kicker (in this example). Usually, these players are betting their hands to be the best hand, since they are in an unraised pot; they are *not* making an "information" bet.

Changing the scenario, suppose the flop comes:

It is an unraised pot. A lot of times, the blind will lead at the pot with second pair, especially if he is holding something such as A-10 offsuit. The small or big blind is the place from which a lot of players will bet second pair in an unraised pot.

With your K-J, you can be fairly sure that you have the best hand and you have the chance to knock your opponent off. I don't suggest raising with the hand; just call. Then if your opponent shuts down on fourth street, you can bet. Or you can play to win just the one bet on the flop. In an unraised pot, there is nothing wrong with just playing to win a small pot on the flop, so that you don't get yourself trapped.

STARTING HANDS BY POSITION

Position is more important in pot-limit and no-limit hold'em than it is in limit hold'em. To play from an early position, you should have an A-Q suited or above. From a middle position, fifth spot and later, you might play A-J or A-10 suited and up. From a late position into the blinds, you can play K-10 suited and above.

Be mindful that a hand such as J-10 suited is rated as a better hand than K-10 suited in a multiway pot. The J-10 gives you more straight possibilities, and because of your kicker, it is easier to get away from if you flop top pair. For example, if the flop comes 10-7-2, your kicker is only a jack, whereas with the K-10, your kicker is the second-highest one that you can have.

But playing hands such as K-9, no. I am not going to play any three-holers such as K-9 or 9-5 or 7-3. Sure, you can flop a straight to these hands, but you can never make the *nut* straight. Although a lot of people play them, I don't play three-holers in hold'em, period.

In poker, the K-9 is called "sawmill." Here's a true story about how it got that name. Cowboy Wolford and Milton Butts were playing up in the hill country in Texas and Cowboy had gotten broke in the game. So, they were driving down a hill going out of town when they passed by a big lumber camp. Cowboy looked over at Milton and said, "Even those guys working in that sawmill wouldn't have got broke on a K-9." And that hand has been called a "sawmill" ever since then.

In a tournament structure, once you get up to the $100-$200 blinds with an ante in no-limit, players will pick up pots with hands like K-9 suited, but in pot-limit tournaments, there never is an ante. Therefore, the idea of picking up pots in pot-limit hold'em tournaments does not have the value that it does in no-limit tourneys because, without the antes, there isn't as much to pick up in pot-limit.

These are opening hands, by position, that Tom and I have been discussing. They are not necessarily hands that you would call with, they are hands that you would open with. Of course, there are other hands that you will play when three or four players are already in the pot, although in unraised pots, it takes pretty much the same standards to call a pot that it does to open it.

RAISING HANDS

The raising hands in pot-limit are the standard raising hands in all of hold'em: aces, kings, on down to A-K. But because pot-limit hold'em is a structured game, if I have a pair of nines or above, I probably will bring in the hand for a minimum raise ($40 in a $10-$10 game). If I get reraised, whether I call depends upon my observation of the players—who does what in which situations. Two nines on a reraise isn't much of a hand; you can always get away from it.

A lot of times, a player will stand a reraise with a pair of nines. If he has brought it in for $40, the reraiser can call the $40 raise and reraise it $100. The three blinds are in for $5, $5, and $10 and you have raised it by $40, making $60 in the pot. Adding the $40 required to call your raise, the reraiser can raise the pot by $100. So, the original raiser often will take a flop with pocket nines because it only costs him $100 more and he might break the reraiser if he flops a set.

You can raise the pot for any amount up to the size of the pot, but I suggest that you always raise the amount of the pot. The only thing that would stop me from raising the size of the pot is if I didn't have enough money in front of me to raise the size of the pot; and in that case, I would raise all-in.

Suppose that Player A has brought it in for a raise and you have called the raise. Then Player C reraises behind you. What do you do? You have all kinds of options. You might be holding two kings and just flat call Player A's raise, but when Player C reraises behind you, you have to decide whether you have the best hand. A lot of times, against average players, your kings will be the best hand and you're going to call Player C's reraise. But you should not take the option of reraising the pot again, because you might be up against two aces.

You also want to see if an ace hits the flop before you commit a lot more money to this pot, so you just flat call before the flop with your kings. If an ace doesn't hit the flop, and if you don't put your opponent(s) on aces, you probably have the best hand—unless somebody flops a set, in which case the action will tell you what to do next.

WHEN NOT TO CALL A RAISE

There are situations when you won't call a raise before the flop. Suppose that Player C raises on the button and one of the blinds pops it again. Unless you have a pair of aces, you probably shouldn't call; you should throw away your kings. You don't have much invested in this pot and even if he doesn't have aces, it's not a bad play to fold the kings. Where I was schooled in Dallas, the second raise probably would have been aces, and the third raise was like Ivory snow: 99.9 percent pure aces. It's not A-K in this situation—it's aces.

Whether you call or fold all gets back to knowing your players. There are players that you know are loose enough to put in the third raise with two queens. But you know that already; so now, your only question is, "Was he lucky enough to pick up two aces in this pot, or do I have the best hand?" Then you make your decision. There are other players that you know would never put in the third raise without two aces, so then it's very easy to dump the two kings. In fact, I dumped them twice against one raise during the World Series of Poker in 1985. I raised the pot, Mike Allen reraised, and I threw them away both times— and both times, Allen showed me two aces.

A world-class player that I know likes to reraise with two queens, because the raise helps him find out where he is. If his opponent mounts him for all his chips, then he knows that his hand is no good. But this reasoning gets back to my theory that you're supposed to know where you're at *without* having to put money in the pot. If you're in a game with a lot of players that you don't know, you should be able to get a line on each of them within the first fifteen minutes of the game. But this type of situation might not come up during that time, so then you just have to make a decision and live with it.

THE PURPOSE OF THE PRE-FLOP ACTION

With a good hand, the purpose of this pre-flop action, remember, is to build a pot. The pre-flop action in no-limit hold'em is much bigger because you can get all of your chips in the pot before the flop, but in pot-limit that usually isn't the case. You might have the same criteria for starting hands in no-limit that you have in pot-limit, but you have to be much more careful with them in no-limit because any time that you play a hand in no-limit, your entire pile of chips is at risk. In pot-limit, it is not. In no-limit side games, a lot more hands are won without seeing a flop than happens in pot-limit side games. That is because you can't put as much pressure on your opponents before the flop in pot-limit games as you can in no-limit games. Therefore, you'll see a lot more flops in pot-limit hold'em.

In no-limit, a three-way pot is somewhat uncommon; usually, it's only two-way action. But in pot-limit hold'em, a lot more people will see the flops, and there will be more multiway pots, especially when you get a lot of players in the game who have a lot of money and are liberal with their pre-flop action. This is what makes the pot-limit side games during a tournament so juicy sometimes. If you make the nuts on these more liberal players, you'll get action from them, whereas in no-limit, you're usually up against just one guy and you won't get the action that you want.

The multiway pot feature of pot-limit hold'em is another reason why you can play the suited connectors and the small pairs more often. That's the whole idea of the game.

THE CHECK-RAISE

Good players always try to maximize their bets in pot-limit to win all that they can get out of a hand. If you're playing check-raise, you're always taking the chance that your opponent won't bet. Then, if you have a big hand, what will you win in that pot?

Therefore, the check-raise is used far more often in no-limit hold'em than it is in pot-limit hold'em.

PLAYING THE BLINDS

A *player* does not stand raises with a weak hand in the blinds; a non-player does. The non-player says to himself, "It's only costing me $30 more (depending on the limits). Since it's only a minimum raise and I have J-10, I'll just call and take off a card." That kind of thinking burns up a lot of money.

You would need to hit the perfect flop to win with a hand such as J-10. Top pair (jacks) is no good because you have no kicker. One of the only two times that you can play the hand is when you know that your opponent makes a token raise with any small pair; then you might look at the flop. If it comes with a jack, you might bet because you know that your opponent is overly aggressive and may have raised with a pair such as threes.

The other time that you can play this hand from the blind is when your opponent is the type of player who always bets on the button when it is checked to him. In this case, you might come back over the top of him from the blind with J-10 and win the pot right there. Of course, every time you do that, you had better be right. And the man on the button has to be a decent player, one that you know will lay down a hand against a raise.

PLAYING ON THE FLOP

The strategy in pot-limit is to build the pot. Always try to maximize the amount of money that you can win when you have a winning hand. Therefore, to slow play on the flop doesn't make much sense, does it?

Say that you flop a big hand and you check on the flop, and all of your opponents also check. The result is that on fourth street, all that you can bet is the amount that you could have bet on the flop. But if you bet on the flop and get a call or two, your next bet can be a pretty good-sized bet. Now you're maximizing what you can win in the pot as you go along with the hand. The art of pot-limit hold'em is knowing how to build the pot. That's the whole idea of the game.

You can slow play hands a lot more in no-limit because you can bet any amount that you want at any time. But in pot-limit, with its structured bets, you have to *build* the amount that you can bet. You're not looking to set a trap with the slow play; you want people to play with you. So, you lead with your sets and hope that somebody will play back at you. If they don't play back, you're hoping that they will at least call because your next bet is going to be larger and you're hoping that they will call again.

As you progress through the betting stages, if your opponents are still with you, you can always bet more as you go along. And that is how you maximize the amount that you can win on the hand.

Suppose you come into a hand with:

The flop comes:

Let's say that you check on the flop. Why would you do that? Are you hoping that someone will bet it for you so that you can put in a raise and shut out your opponent? Wrong!

If you lead with the hand, nobody will know for sure what you have. If someone flat calls you, that's OK because he doesn't know where you're at, and you're getting more money into the pot so that you can lead at it again.

Or, somebody might raise you, in which case your best play (with the king on the board) may be to just call — not because you're afraid that he has trip kings, but because you don't want to blow him out of the pot. You still want to build that pot!

If you are raised and you just flat call, then on fourth street there is some good money in the pot. Now you might want to check, let him make the bet, and then go over the top of him with a raise. Now you have him pot-committed.

Of course, there are a lot of ways to play any hand, but when you have a big hand, always keep in mind that your goal is to maximize what you can win in the pot. You don't want to take the chance of flopping a big hand and just winning $40 with it. That happens a lot of times, and sometimes you can't help it: You lead and they throw their hands away, so all you win is what is in the pot.

Another reason that you want to lead at the pot with your jacks against the K♣ J♣ 4♠ flop is that you don't want to give your opponents a cheap draw at you. With a couple of suited connectors, someone could easily have a wrap-around straight draw or a flush draw. So, you want to make them put some money in the pot to make their draws, make them pay to play. Then if the possible straight or flush comes, you can always get away from your hand.

In no-limit hold'em, you can distort the size of the pot with your bets, making it unprofitable for your opponent to play the draw. In pot-limit, you can't do that as much but you still can make it expensive enough that your opponents won't be able to draw at you cheaply. A big part of your strategy in pot-limit is to manipulate the size of the pot with your bets.

PLAYING SECOND PAIR IN LATE POSITION

Suppose that a couple of players have checked on the flop, you have second-pair, and it's up to you. I don't suggest that you bet it right there. You can take off another card and get a little more information on the hand without putting any money into the pot. Believe me, another card will give you a lot more information, and you won't be taking any chances in case you're playing against guys who like to check raise.

As Tom says, "If you know that your opponents are likely to check raise and lay traps, you are less likely to bet than if they are playing straightforwardly, in which case you have more reason to bet. It all goes back to knowing your opponents."

TOP PAIR, BIG KICKER

Your biggest worry in pot-limit hold'em is getting broke in an unraised pot. But if you flop top pair with top kicker in an unraised pot, you have to put in a bet. Say that you have A-9 suited or offsuit, you're in one of the blinds, and you can get in cheaply.

Your hand:

The flop comes:

Even from a front position, you have to bet your hand, because in an unraised pot, there is better than a 75 percent chance that you have the best hand. The only thing that you have to worry about is that someone has limped into the pot (probably from one of the blinds, since it is an unraised pot) with two deuces or fives and flops a set or two pair.

A player also could have a 3-4 suited, but you would like that. First of all, you have the ace in your hand, which is one of his straight cards. Secondly, any time that you are a 2-to-1 favorite in a hand, you want your opponents to draw. If they make it, they make it, but you have the best of it. So, with the type of flop mentioned above, you definitely want to lead bet with your A-9.

We are specifically discussing the A-9 because with this type of hand, you are likely to just limp in with it in an unraised pot if there are a bunch of limpers in front of you. But now suppose that you have an A-Q in the blind and there are a lot of limpers in the pot. With the A-Q, you probably would want to raise.

When you flop top pair and big kicker, you don't necessarily have to have the top kicker to lead bet. Say the flop comes 9-5-2 and you have Q-9 in your hand. Since you got in the pot for nothing, you can lead bet. You're not leading to find out information; you're leading to win the pot, you're betting it as the best hand. There is a big difference in betting your hand as the best hand, and betting "to find out where you are at."

Now suppose that you are holding the A-9, the flop comes 9-5-2, you bet, and you get called.

Your hand:

A king comes on the turn.

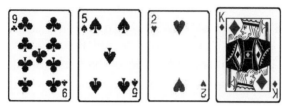

Should that scare you? No, not in either pot-limit or no-limit. If you were called on the flop, it probably means that somebody had something with the nine; a draw, or maybe even a pair in a rank between the fives and nines (a pair of sevens, for example). Unless a player had a K-5 or K-9, why would he have called you? And if you were holding the Q-9 (as in the second example above), you were already beaten anyway.

In limit hold'em, that king on the turn would scare you to death, but in pot-limit and no-limit, it wouldn't. A much scarier card on the turn would be a connected card to the nine, a ten or an eight, because someone could have limped in with a 10-9 or a 9-8 suited to make two pair on the turn. Even a jack on the turn would be scarier than a king. Anything that connects within two holes of the ten would be scary because most pot-limit players will play a one-holer (J-9 or Q-10, for example) or a two-holer (J-8 or Q-9), especially in tournaments, but they will not play a three-holer (Q-8 or J-7).

WALKING BACK TO HOUSTON: PLAYING BIG SLICK

It's two hundred and forty-nine miles from Dallas to Houston. We used to say that if you play Big Slick often enough in Dallas and you live in Houston, you're gonna' have to walk back to Houston a few times—and for a good reason. In both pot-limit and no-limit hold'em, ace-king is the type of hand that you want to win without seeing a flop. You raise with the hand, yes, but you raise *because* you want to win the money right then and there.

Suppose you are holding:

The flop comes:

You usually would lead at the pot in this situation, but there are a few occasions when you might slow play the hand. Although we have said that you never slow play in pot-limit hold'em, actually we should never say *never*, because even in pot-limit, there are exceptions to the rule.

For example, suppose that you have raised the pot before the flop. There are weaker players who will call the pot with hands such as K-Q, K-J, or K-10. Why not give them one check—you know that they will come right out of their shoes if they flop top pair—and then you can get them with a check-raise. But if you are going to check raise, you must *do it on the flop* so that you don't give your opponents a chance to make a second pair or anything else on the turn.

Over the years, so many players have said, "How could you get broke with one pair?" That is why you check raise on the flop, without giving them a chance at making a double pair or some fantastic drawout on the turn. There are ten cards that are connected to the king, and they could be playing a queen, jack, a 10, or with some bad players, even a nine. So, when you check, they may figure, "Well, he's got something between tens and kings, so I'd better take this pot right now." Then you've got 'em!

So much of this strategy depends upon the texture of the flop and the nature of the players at the table. Just be sure that you know your opponents well enough that you figure one of them will bet on the flop so that you can put in your check-raise. The whole idea is to get them pot-committed.

Any time that you have the top hand, you want to get your opponent committed to the pot. If you have the A-K, and the flop comes K-Q, you're a little afraid of it, but you still bet it. You realize that if he plays back at you, you're still trying to catch a card, most of the time ... unless your opponent is a weak player. If the flop comes K-Q, your opponent might be holding K-Q or J-10. It's even possible that he might call you with A-10, hoping to catch the gut-shot straight on the turn.

PLAYING DRAWS

What's the use in playing a draw if you can't get it paid off when you make it? That is the fallacy in playing draws in pot-limit and no-limit. Against a top player, if the flop comes with two of a suit and you call a bet, and then if the third card to your suit comes on the turn and you bet your flush, the top player won't pay you off. You are a 4.5-to-1 underdog to make the draw with one card to come, and if you are successful in making your hand, you aren't going to win any more money with it anyway.

So, if you decide to make the draw, the only way to play it is to put in a pot-sized bet to get enough money into the pot to make it worth your while to draw to it. The only way that making such a draw makes sense is to do it against weaker players, because they will pay you off on the end. Straight draws can be harder for your opponents to read than flush draws, so you might prefer drawing to a straight than drawing to a flush.

PLAYING BOTTOM TWO PAIR

In a pot-limit game that I played a few years ago, five players were in for $40 each. I had the Q♥ J♥ and I was getting big odds for my money, so I called on the button. The flop came J-7-8 with two hearts. It was pass, pass, bet, and I raised. I had top pair, an overcard, and a flush draw. One of the guys beat me into the pot with his call. Then the board ragged off on fourth street. I had begun the hand with $850 and I had around $300 left; I wasn't going to dog the hand at that point so I came at it again. On the river, I missed everything; I still just had top pair. My opponent won the hand with 8-7 offsuit. But on the flop, my hand was favored over 8-7 offsuit, the bottom two pair.

Bottom two pair in both pot-limit and no-limit hold'em is a treacherous hand. A lot of players forget that there is such a thing as a running pair. For example, the board could have come with a four on the turn and another four on the river, making eights and sevens for my opponent in this scenario, and jacks and fours for me.

As Tom reminds us, you have to protect your hand if you have bottom two pair. You should do whatever you can to win it on the flop. I had multiple ways to win the pot: nine hearts, two jacks, and three queens, times two (two draws), plus the possibility of a running pair—32 ways to make the hand, including the running pair. In Dallas, we used to call 28 outs with two to come an even hand. In Houston, they called 24 outs an even hand.

Plus, when you are doing the betting, you have even more of an edge. And even though you might lose the pot (as I did), you should always get your money in correctly. A lot of times, you might win the pot right on the flop with your bet. And even if your opponent double pairs and calls or raises your bet, you're still a slight favorite with two cards to come.

Tom points out, too, that if a player flops bottom two pair, it might be correct for him to continue with the hand. "He already has put a lot of money into the pot if it was raised before the flop, and so it becomes correct for him to keep playing the hand, just as it is correct for the player with top pair/top kicker to continue. Even if he is a slight dog, he isn't much more of a dog than the other hand. Many times, then, it is correct for both players to go to the center."

Here is an amendment to this story. When the game started, I had $1,000 and when this hand came up, I had $850 that I was jeopardizing in the play of this hand. But if you had $5,000 in front of you, or even $3,000, you might play the hand completely differently. With a big bankroll, you might trail with this hand all the way. If you don't hit on fourth street, and your opponent is an aggressive player, he will put the test to you. Then, what are you going to do? You only have one card to come to hit the hand; one-half of your outs are gone. But with a short amount of money in a raised pot such as this one, the gamble is well worth it.

You see, when you have more money, you have more reason to protect your stack, especially in a tournament. With less money, you might be more likely to gamble because your risk is limited.

In a tournament, in fact, I would never make the play that I did, because it isn't smart to jeopardize your whole stack in an even-money situation. Also, you wouldn't be playing the Q♥ J♥ in a tournament; you wouldn't even call the original bet with it. Tom suggests, however, that he would play the hand in a rebuy tournament, or in the early stages of any tournament, if he is on the button with it and only has to call a small bet with the hand. So there are at least two ways of looking at this situation.

The scenario changes depending upon the circumstances: At a four-handed table in a tournament, you might play the hand aggressively against the flop mentioned earlier, because four-handed, you don't necessarily need to have a big hand or a big flop. As Tom points out, in shorthanded tournament action, people are attacking the blinds all of the time, and they don't need big hands to do that. "If I flop top pair and a flush draw against one opponent (who doesn't have to have a big hand to be in the pot), I very likely will come over the top of him right on the flop." So, if you play this hand shorthanded in a tournament, you play it aggressively from the flop onward, or you don't play it at all.

The situation when you would play Q-J suited in a

tournament is when the opening raise is a small one, you have a lot of chips in front of you, and you're trying to knock your opponent out of the tournament. When you make your original call, you're not thinking, "I have the best hand with a queen-high."

If you get the top-pair/flush-draw flop, you have to play it aggressively, the way that I played the hand with short money.

Tom explains: "Many times, you know that you don't have the best hand going in, but you have a hand that has some potential. With the huge implied odds in pot-limit, remember that you don't have to start with the best hand all of the time. It all depends on whether you think that you can outplay your opponent, or that you will be paid off if you hit your hand."

Obviously, the number of players at your table has a lot of impact on the hands that you play in a tournament. Most tournaments today start with a ten-handed table, but we used to start with eleven players in Dallas — believe me, it takes a much bigger hand to win an eleven-handed game than it does to win a four-handed game. This applies even more to ring games than it does to tournaments. The optimal field for a pot-limit or no-limit game or tournament table is eight-handed because you have a lot more maneuverability in the way that you play and in your hand selection.

The more people in the game, the bigger the hand it takes to win; the fewer people, the smaller the hand it takes to win. Fullhanded, you have to give more respect to your opponents. Shorthanded, things get down to the nuts and bolts of the game, and that is when you find out what kind of player you are, especially in tournaments.

The point is that your play changes dramatically depending upon the number of players in the game. As Tom summarized, you have to be more cognizant of the quality of your hands in a full ring game, whereas in shorthanded play, you have to be more cognizant of the quality of your opponents. This brings to mind once again that there are a lot of players who have the skill to *get to* the final table, but there are very few who have the skill to *play* the final table.

Both Tom and I have been approached by no less than one hundred players who have asked us, "What am I doing wrong? I get there, but I never win." The bottom line is that they haven't honed their shorthanded skills well enough. As Tom says, "Here is where I think people falter: They don't know the value of their hands, as hand values change dramatically in shorthanded play. And they don't seize situations properly."

In Latin, *carpe diem*: means "Seize the day." You have to do that to win a tournament.

PLAYING BIG PAIRS

The three hands that knock more people out of pot-limit tournaments than any other ones are a pair of queens, a pair of jacks, or ace-king.

Suppose you have:

The flop comes:

If you have two queens and the flop comes with either a king or an ace, I think that you should be ready to give it up. If you are going to win the pot (with the king or ace on the board), you want to win it in a showdown; you don't want to put any money in the pot.

If you're against only one opponent with your pair of queens and the flop comes something like K-7-4, Tom will bet the pot in an attempt to win it right there. If his opponent has a king in his hand, obviously Tom won't be successful, but at least he hasn't given the man a chance to hit an ace, in case he has one in the hole with a card other than a king (an A-J or A-Q, for example). I wouldn't make a play at this pot myself, but that is the difference in our approaches.

My thinking is that if I am playing in a pot that I have raised before the flop, it is likely that my opponent(s) will have the overcard if it comes on the flop. The idea of betting to find out where you are in the hand just doesn't make sense to me in this scenario, whether the pot is multiway or two-handed.

My theory is that if my opponent bets on the flop, I can make a decision about whether he has a hand, but if I bet into him, I take the chance of getting raised. If my hand is the best one on the flop, there is a good chance that another overcard is not going to come out. Now, I have my information without losing any money. So, you can bet the hand on fourth street, if you want to, or you can play it to show it down. But why lose money in the pot? There is already enough in the pot to win some real money, so why bet it again?

Suppose that you are in front position with the pair of queens, you check, and your opponent bets. Ask yourself, "Who am I playing this pot against? Is my opponent a guy who would bet an underpair, or would he need top pair to bet?" Since you have played with him for a while, you should know the answer. I believe that you will make more money in this situation by checking than you will ever make by leading because you can get yourself in a trap by betting the hand.

Now, suppose that you check and your opponent also checks. You pretty well know that yours is the best hand, because if he wanted to trap you in this situation, he would be trapping you with a big hand. If he had a king with a decent kicker, he would bet it, but if he flopped a set, he would let you come to him because you were the original aggressor.

Suppose that my opponent is sitting in front of me and I am sitting behind him with the queens. The flop again comes K-rag-rag, and he checks it to me. Whether I would bet in this situation depends on what I know about my opponent. If an aggressive player such as Tom checks to me, I probably would bet it, but I am still not going to get broke to this hand, no matter what.

What happens if you bet and get called? Even though you've made the bet, you can still shut down. Your opponent might be holding K-rag in the big blind, for example, and wouldn't bet the hand, but he might call you with it.

You never know what some players will call a raise with from the big blind, especially when it is shorthanded in a tournament. If it's down to four or five players in a tournament, a player might call a raise with a rag ace or a rag king.

Many times, players will call with hands such as K-5 suited, "The Broke's Lament." Of course, *you* are not going to play that way, but some other players do.

The Broke's Lament: Suited big card-rag such as K-5

HITTING A SET ON THE FLOP

When you hit your set of queens on the flop, how you play the hand depends on how many players have called your raise before the flop. Say that you raised and had three callers: In this case, you can lead with the hand and just pray that they play back at you. If there are a couple of connectors on the flop, especially if they are suited, you have all the more reason to bet the pot. And if you are playing against super aggressive players, you definitely want to bet because they will often bluff at you, or will call with an underpair. You want to get these types of players to commit money to the pot as soon as possible. After all, three queens is a big hand.

Say that you raised the pot before the flop, nobody reraised, and the flop comes A-K-Q. You are still the favorite to win the pot, although in smaller pot-limit games, you might also run into a player holding J-10. Still, I would lead at the pot, hoping that someone has flopped aces and kings. You can't be afraid to bet, always thinking that the nut hand is out against you.

WHEN YOU FLOP AN OVERPAIR

What do you do if you are holding queens in a raised pot with two callers, the flop comes J♣ 8♣ 2♣, and you are *not* holding the queen of clubs?

Your hand:

The flop comes:

Tom would play the hand this way: "If I am first to act with only two opponents, my queens probably are the best hand, unless someone has flopped a lucky flush. A more likely hand for an opponent to be holding is something like the A♣ J♥, with a draw to the nut flush. With only two opponents, I am going to lead at the pot; however, against four opponents, the two queens (an overpair) are much more vulnerable. If I am first to act, I will just check, but if I am last to act, I will bet."

Say that you have an opponent who never reraises with A-K (which isn't a bad play on his part because you can get yourself into a trap with A-K). Again, the flop comes J♣ 8♣ 2♣. What do you do in this situation? You don't know whether your opponent has A-K, but it is a likely hand for him to be holding. He could have the A♣K♦, making you an underdog in this hand. In that case, he would have 28 outs, including nine clubs, three aces (if he has the A♣), and two kings, making his hand about even-money. How you play the hand against this opponent goes back to the first chapter on knowing your opponents, the most important skill in big-bet poker.

Now, let's take a look at a different scenario. Suppose you are holding:

Again, the flop comes:

As for me, if I were holding the A♣ 10♠ (for example) against the J♣ 8♣ 2♣ flop, I would never call a bet, *never*. In pot-limit and no-limit, when I have two of a suit in my hand and two of my suit come on the flop, it always seems to me that I have a better chance of making the hand than when the flop comes suited and I have one of the board suit in my hand.

Of course, the odds are exactly the same in either scenario, but I don't draw for the fourth suited card to come on the board. As Tom says, how am I going to get any action, anyway, if the fourth club comes on the board? But when I have two of the suit in my hand and a *third* suited card falls on the board, I may get action when I bet the flush. An intermediate or novice player who holds one of the board suit might still draw for the fourth suited card to hit the board, but I think that is an error.

PLAYING POCKET ACES

Obviously, pocket aces is the best hand that you can start with. The only time that I would ever limp with aces is in a very aggressive game, because in an aggressive game when you limp with aces, one guy might raise, then this one calls, that one calls ... and you can turn the aces into a powerhouse by coming over the top of them. You can eliminate a lot of the players that way, and if you get called, you know that you have the best hand going in. Then, it's just Lady Luck's call from the flop onward.

Another way of playing aces is to bring them in for a raise and hope that someone reraises you. If you're against only one opponent, you just flat call the reraise. Then if the board comes with rags, you're in good shape. The only time that you should be afraid is when the board comes with kings, queens, or jacks, because your opponent could have been raising with pocket pairs of these ranks and flop a set. If the flop comes K-Q-J, you can dump the aces in a flash if your opponent comes out swinging at you, without anyone knowing that you held pocket aces (since you only flat called the raise).

But when the flop is a split board, you can really trap a single opponent well because you didn't reraise him; you didn't shut him out before the flop.

If you're playing in a normal game, you usually bring it in for a raise with pocket aces because, although you want to make money with them, you don't want to have seven people drawing at your aces. Even though the aces are still the favorite, they are not a big favorite with that many people in the pot. The worst scenario when you hold pocket aces is this: Say that you're playing in a $10-$10 game and you can only raise $40 from the first seat with your aces, and you get six callers—all of whom have pocket pairs. This could happen!

I was in a pot once in Dallas when the flop came with the Q♦ 10♦ 5♦. One player had the nut flush and the other three each flopped a set. The turn and river came with a running pair of fours and the queens-full won the pot. The worst player in the hand was able to get away from the three tens because of the amount of money being moved at the pot. So, the worst possible scenario when you have pocket aces is for everybody who calls you to be holding a pair — Any broken board in the world can come, and somebody will flop a set. But you know that this is a possibility coming in, and that is why you raise before the flop to limit the number of your opponents.

Suppose that you are holding:

The flop comes:

How do you play trip aces in this scenario? Tom says that he likes to lead with the aces in this situation. "The only thing that I'm worried about is the K-Q, and even then I'm not dead. What you don't want to do is let people draw at you for free, because if a king or a queen slips off the deck, it is very possible that someone will make a straight.

So, you want to take the lead against this dangerous flop and if you are raised, you probably will want to move in on the raiser. Frankly, I might get broke with this hand." Tom is right: Anybody, including me, might go broke with this hand.

The perfect flop, the one that you want to see when you have pocket aces, is A-K-rag, A-Q-rag, or A-J-rag. Somebody might be holding any two of the top cards and make two pair on the flop. Oh boy, do I like to lead with this type of flop! As Tom analyzes it, "You want your opponent to have an ace in his hand because he can't give you any action unless he has an ace or has flopped a set. You definitely want to lead at the pot because you don't want to give your opponent the chance to make a belly-straight on the turn."

However, I never lead at it with that thought in mind; I lead at the pot thinking, "Oh, baby, I know he's flopped two pair and he's going to play back at me!"

Now, suppose the same type of flop comes, except that two of the cards are suited:

This is another flop that you want to lead at with pocket aces, because you want your opponents to play back at you. If they make their flush or straight, so what? You're still a big favorite in the hand with your three aces.

As Tom says, "Leading at the pot in pot-limit or no-limit always makes sense because if your opponents hit the flop with two pair, they can't get away from it and you can build a giant pot for yourself, especially if they raise when you bet. Then you know that you have them by the throat because they have made a substantial commitment to the pot, and they will have to make a straight or a flush to beat you if they have drawing hands.

"A lot of times, if you check, your opponent bets, and then you raise, he will lay down his hand, because you're tipping off the strength of your hand. But if you lead at the pot, the ordinary player (a beginning or intermediate player) will seldom give you credit for having the nuts."

Say that the flop comes A-Q-J, you are sitting in last position, and a player leads at the pot. Now what do you do with your trip aces? It all depends. I am a chance taker, and I like to win big pots, so I may just smooth call him on the flop and wait until fourth street to make my move. Of course, you can lose the pot if the wrong card comes off, but Columbus took a chance, so why not you too?

PLAYING ON THE TURN

On the turn in pot-limit hold'em, you still want to build the pot if you have a hand. And again, I suggest that you always bet the size of the pot because you never want to tip off your opponents one iota about the value of your hand. If I have a made hand, I usually will still lead at the pot, unless I'm playing against a loosey-goosey type of player who gives a lot of action. In that case, I may check the hand and let him come at me.

Tom says that against this type of loose player, he may change the size of his bet—bet only three-quarters of the pot, for example. That approach also has some value. But suppose there are five good players in the game and four not-so-good players. When you're in a pot with the five good players, are you going to make a full bet, and then when you're in with the four other players, are you going to make a lesser bet?

I believe that if you reduce your bet size with some of them, you have to do it with all of them, or else you're going to tip the value of your hand. And I never want to tip the strength of my hand one iota.

I understand that Tom is talking about varying his bet size in a head-up situation against a loose player, but the other players are still sitting in the game—and you're going to be playing hands with those other guys, too. What are you going to do, tip them off that when you underbet the pot, you have a big hand, and when you bet the size of the pot, you don't? I don't believe that you should do that because the underbet that you make in the hand against a loose opponent is only one hand among many hands that you're going to be playing. I don't want to give the good players a tell that I underbet the pot when I have a hand—unless I'm trying to put a reverse tell on them.

What I'm looking at is the big picture of the game. One hand is only a small part of the puzzle and I don't want to give away any pieces of the puzzle by the way that I play one hand because the good players will pick up on it. Good players pick up on everything.

Think of the big picture all of the time while you are playing.

DRAWING HANDS

Now suppose that you have a draw. On the flop, you might want to bet your draw because you have two chances to win: They might throw their hands away, or you might catch your card on the turn and make a big hand. On fourth street, however, I wouldn't bet the draw. The main thing to realize about drawing hands is that you must be in position to play them.

Suppose that you're in early position with a draw on the flop, and it doesn't get there on the turn. Can you lead at this hand again? No, you can't. Your opponents are going to detect that you're on a drawing hand and they're going to try to take the pot. But if you're in position on a drawing hand—the other guys are in front of you—then you can bet your draw. The only time that you can bet a draw is when you are *behind* the other players, when they check to you on the flop and you bet. Then on fourth street, they still have to act first.

By betting the draw on the flop, if they check to you on fourth street, then you can also check and get a free card, similar to limit hold'em.

The difference is that in limit play, you have to raise

to get that free card, whereas in pot-limit, you play position to get a free card. In pot-limit and no-limit when you're in late position and you're on a draw, one of the worst things that you can do is bet a draw on fourth street, with one card to come, after everybody has checked to you. You could have gotten the draw for nothing!

Furthermore, if you bet on the turn, you're opening it up for them to raise you and shut you out of making your draw. I don't mind making the bet on the flop and opening it to a raise because then I have two cards to come. If someone does raise on the flop, then I can decide whether I want to play the draw or fold right there.

Also, I'm not saying that you always have to bet your draw on the flop from a late position. Sometimes, you might decide to just check. But remember, what's the use of making a drawing hand and not winning any money with it? Tom also notes that there is the deception factor when you bet your draw on the flop. Your opponents can't be sure of what type of hand you have; they may not guess that you're on a draw.

By betting on the flop, you may win the pot right there. In pot-limit, your options are better when you bet the draw than when you don't bet it.

If you bet a draw in early position and it doesn't get there, you're throwing up a white flag. You can't bet it on fourth street when it doesn't get there. Why? Because if you do bet it, you're committing a lot of money with only one card to come. You also might get raised, and then what do you do?

The cardinal sin in pot-limit is betting that draw *again* on fourth street, opening yourself up to a raise. In fact, some of the good players might put you on a draw and raise with nothing just to shut you out of the pot!

So, you can bet your draw on the flop from a late position when you're last to act, but not from a front spot. When you're in late position, if an opponent makes something on the turn and bets into you, you can always get away from the hand if you haven't made it. Plus, you might have made a big hand, in which case you may want to check it along on fourth street. Then, let them come at you on fifth street, where you can put a raise on them. Being in that late position gives you lots of options.

THE BLUFF

We all bluff, but nobody can bluff a weak player. That would be like committing suicide. Anytime you try to bluff calling stations, they are likely to call you with the worst possible hands that you can imagine. All they know about is what they have: They never think about what anybody else is holding.

Occasionally, though, you *can* bluff a weak player, but only in certain situations. Say that you have a lot of chips and he doesn't have very many chips. If you bluff at this man, you have put it to him that if he calls and is wrong in making the call, he is out of the tournament. Your bet says, "You'd better be right, because if you're wrong you're out of action." This type of bluff is used a lot by strong players because they know that it is very hard for the calling station to make the call under these circumstances. They may have been calling stations all along, but when it jeopardizes all of their chips, they suddenly get scared.

However, this is a situation in which you would *not* bluff a good player because a strong player will pick it off in a New York minute. Therefore, I never try this type of bluff against a good player. For example, one year at the World Series of Poker deep into the tournament (the third day of the Championship no-limit hold'em event), the action was passed to Berry Johnston who held the K♥ 8♥ on the button. He brought it in for a raise, trying to pick up the blinds. Tommy Grimes had an A-Q behind him and came over the top of him. But Berry had one-half of his chips in the pot and decided that he wasn't going to give it up. He caught an eight to win the pot and then he went on to win the tournament. This was the key hand for him. The point is that you just don't mess with a top player unless you've got the goods.

THE BIG BLUFF

The best bluff is the big bluff. When somebody is trying to take a shot at you, you come back over the top of him — this is the resteal, or the rebluff. Tom explains that "You can try to resteal when you think that a player is out of line. Maybe he's been bringing in a lot of pots for raises, and he doesn't always have premium hands when he does it. So now, you might decide to gamble with that A-J that you might have mucked against a solid player's raise from early position."

You can make a strong rebluff by waiting until later in the hand. For example, you might not even hold a pair, but you know from the way that the action is taking place that the raiser is swinging at the pot. You might try to take it away from him on fourth or fifth street, rather than on the flop, because you want a little bit of money in the pot to make it worth your while.

I once tried a resteal in a limit hold'em tournament

when I knew that my opponent was out of line. I brought it in for a raise with the K♠ J♠. The flop came 9♠ 8♦ 4♠, giving me two overs and a flush draw. The big blind check-raised me on the turn when a nothing-card came off. He could have had a variety of hands, but I flat called him. On fifth street, the board paired with nines. The big blind checked to me, and I bet. Then he raised. And although I had missed everything and only had two overcards, I came back over the top of him again. He mucked his hand.

I am not suggesting that you ever try this play in limit hold'em, but in almost every tournament that I have won, I have made at least one grandstand play. Luckily, I have been right about 95 percent of the time. But once in a while, in pot-limit or no-limit ring games as well as in tournaments, you can make this play when you put a guy on a weak hand, because there is enough money in the pot so that you can really send it to him. Just because I am the type of player who likes to lead at pots in pot-limit doesn't mean that everybody does. A lot of players don't like to do that.

PLAYING ON THE RIVER

Tom talks about how he plays the river in pot-limit. "Suppose that you are involved in a multiway pot on the river. If two or three players have been contesting the pot, it is probable that at least one of them has a drawing hand. If a scare card comes on the river that looks as though it might complete a drawing hand, I might just turn over my cards without a bet if the action is checked to me, even if I have top set. So, I will be somewhat selective in what I bet if a scare card comes on the river.

If a scare card doesn't come on the river, I will go ahead and bet if I think that I have the best hand, even if it's only top pair with top kicker. Sometimes, a player will try to trap me on the river, but he usually will have sprung his trap sooner than the river card (though not always). If someone has put me on a draw, he will usually make his play on fourth street because he doesn't want me to be drawing. Therefore, I am less worried about a trap on the river when a blank comes than I am when a scare card comes, and I will go ahead and value bet if I think that I have the best hand.

If I bet on the river when a blank comes off and then somebody raises me, I will have to reevaluate my hand. It becomes a question of judgment, based on what I know about the player. (Or in a tournament, it may be a decision that is based on chip position.) The strength of my hand also influences my decision. One-pair hands that are check raised at the river are usually very vulnerable, though not always. It depends somewhat on the player, whether he is somebody who will take a shot at you."

Certain players will try to win a hand from you on the river with a stone bluff. But you should know who they are, and part of that depends on just how things come up, how the hand is played. If you have been a player for a long time, you will notice that, over the years, your first instincts are correct up to 98 percent of the time. Those instincts cannot be taught; they come from thousands of hours of playing. Whenever you go against them, you're trying to figure out some way in which this or that scenario could come up. In essence, you start talking yourself out of something. You're scaring yourself.

It's like the guy who calls on the end: He figures out a hand that he can beat and then he puts his opponent on that hand—not the hand the man has, but the hand that he can beat. He does this to justify calling the bet. People do this all the time. In limit hold'em, it's the worst thing in the world to do, because at the end of the day, the bets that you save on the end will probably add up to what you win for the day. If you can win three or more bets an hour in limit poker, that's a pretty nice deal. But in pot-limit and no-limit, you're looking to win a lot more than that.

If you get stuck in pot-limit and no-limit hold'em, especially no-limit, you can get even on one hand if you have a bankroll. Or you can get winner on one hand. You can be $5,000 stuck, put $10,000 in the pot, win one hand, and suddenly you're a $5,000 winner. In pot-limit, if you use the strategy that we have been talking about—maximizing the pot—you can get even quickly if you're stuck, or come from behind to win. But once you get buried in limit hold'em, you have to win a whole lot of hands to get even. And it's hard, it's *really* hard, to do that.

In addition to having judgment and experience, the players who can maximize the pot in pot-limit and no-limit hold'em are the better players. That's what makes them the better players. When it comes down to the end where you have to decide whether to bet the hand or check it, the better player will *know* whether or not he has the best hand, and he will get a bet out of it in situations where the lesser player will not.

Theoretically, the cards break even in the long run, even though there will be fluctuations in the short run and over a lifetime, some players will be slightly luckier than others. But I maintain that the top player not only will beat you with *his* cards, he will beat you with *your* cards. He will win more with your cards than you will, and he will lose less with them. Poker is a game of mistakes, especially tournament poker.

4

HOW TO WIN POT-LIMIT HOLD'EM TOURNAMENTS

The World Series of Poker made some significant changes in format in 1996. Before that time, all of the $1,500 pot-limit tournaments began with $10-$25 limits, but in '96 the events began with limits of $25-$50. This change essentially eliminated the first round of play and caused the tournaments to begin at what formerly had been the second round, thus making the play move much faster. Tournament officials made the change because of the large number of entries in the event; they wanted to get it over with faster so that the tournament wouldn't have to go to a two-day format.

In 1997, the entry fee rose from $1,500 to $2,000, which meant that players had more chips to start with, and which made starting the blinds at $25-$50 more acceptable. Tournament officials also decided to go to a two-day format for both the $2,000 (formerly the $1,500) and the $3,000 (formerly the $2,500) pot-limit hold'em events, as well as all of the other tournaments in the Series, except for the four-day-long $10,000 championship event.

Even though this is a slightly faster format than the top players like, the additional $500 in chips somewhat compensates for it. Still, the $25-$50 beginning blinds are fairly high compared to the number of chips that you start with in the $2,000 tournament. The more time that you have to play (the longer the rounds or the smaller the blinds), the better it is for top players. Loose and aggressive players prefer faster formats with shorter rounds and higher blinds. The more chips that the top players have to play with in relationship to the size of the blinds, the more opportunities they have to outmaneuver and outplay the lesser players.

TYPES OF PLAYERS

Four different categories of players enter pot-limit hold'em tournaments. There are players like Freddy Deeb and Stu Ungar who are super aggressive; they are going to play more hands than the whole table will play combined. They stand raises with hands that a lot of players would fold. They either amass a lot of chips or they're out of the tournament.

Then there are the semi-aggressive players. I classify myself in this category. I am very aggressive late in the tournament, but am semi-aggressive in the middle stages. There are also passive players and defensive players. The passive player will play pots but he never leads at the pot. Usually, he's playing from behind, letting somebody else bet for him. If he has a K-10 in his hand and the board comes K-10-8, he doesn't lead with the hand, and then he doesn't raise on the flop if somebody else bets. He's afraid that a queen or a jack is going to come off on the turn and make a straight for somebody. He doesn't get full value from his hands. He may last a long time, but he never gets enough chips to win the event.

The defensive player is usually a scared player. He becomes intimidated by playing at a table with known players. You know he's afraid even before the cards are dealt. I hear it a lot: "Oh no, don't tell me I have to play at the table with so-and-so." Defensive players don't usually make it to the final table, and if you're a strong player, you have them at a disadvantage even before the tournament begins. You know that in the right spot, you can make them lay down a hand.

PERFECT TOURNAMENT STRATEGY

The perfect tournament strategy is to work towards increasing your chips at the end of every level of play They don't need to increase by any specified amount, but they always need to multiply. This is the perfect scenario, because it shows that you are playing a steady brand of poker.

A lot of players can make the final table, but there are very few who really know how to *play* the final table. That's why you see the same faces most of the time at the final table in pot-limit and no-limit hold'em. A lot more skill is involved in these games than in other ones.

EARLY STAGE

With the opening blinds at $25-$50, the first player in the pot can just call $50 or he can call $50 and raise $125 the amount that is in the pot (including his $50 call)—

meaning that he can come in for $175. After that, the play is straight pot-limit. The next player can call the $175 and raise for a $525 total bet. The action goes like this all the way around the circle.

Remember that in tournament poker, you have to survive to have a chance to win. Even though some people may be playing crazy and a few players are winning a lot of chips, you must still have only one goal in your mind at all times—winning the tournament. You can't win it in the first hour, or in the first two or three hours. You have to outlast the other players. Because of this, you don't want to open up too much during the first three, four, or five hours of the tournament. You want to play solid and let the others make mistakes. You will be playing your perfect ring-game strategy.

DRAWS

The good players stay away from draws, although there are situations in which you must play a draw. Say that you have raised the pot with the following:

The board comes 10-7-2 with two hearts.

Follow the old stud strategy: You don't draw at a flush unless you have two overcards to the board and are drawing to the nut flush. When you have two overcards and the nut-flush draw, you have a huge hand; in fact, it is the only type of flush draw that I want to play because the hand has so many outs (you can hit either one of the overcards or make the flush to win).

Playing a common flush draw in the early stages of the tournament is foolish. Some weaker players will get involved with a flush draw and will put one-half of their chips in the pot with their chances of making the flush only 1-in-3. Sometimes, they will make the flush and still lose to the nut flush. This is a common mistake that a lot of players make, but one that the top players *never* make.

It is almost always these weak players who put the beats on you, not the strong players who are playing sensibly. Of course, if it weren't for weak players, we wouldn't have such huge overlays in the WSOP. But it's very frustrating to see a bad player make a bad play — say, put all of his money in with the 9♥ 8♥, get there, and knock you off at the river, when he shouldn't have been drawing to the hand at all. You know that this type of player has zero chance of winning the tournament, but he has totally eliminated *your* chances.

Another thing that is frustrating is that those players usually take other people down with them. Say that you're in a three-way pot with a pretty decent hand. If you have a hand that you need to play, you can get caught in the middle and get knocked off by a lesser hand.

THE MAZE

I think that you should treat tournament poker like you would a maze that has nothing but trap doors all over the place. You always have to be careful to stay out of those traps. Thinking along these lines should come as second nature to you. Be an offensive poker player who plays defense naturally.

If you don't have anything at all on the flop, somebody can pick up on that and be sharp enough to shut you out on the turn. But if you don't take the first card off with a mediocre hand, you won't waste a lot of chips. Once again, play *survival*. In the flush-draw discussed above, you don't let anybody shut you out because you're the one who's putting the money in the pot. You fully commit yourself to the hand.

In the early stages, you don't want to make a lot of sudden moves; you just have to play a patient, controlled game while looking for a few openings. While you should play more conservatively in the opening rounds, you don't need to play so tight that you don't take any risks.

MIDDLE STAGE

There is no cut and dried formula as to when you start opening up your play in a tournament. You have to size up the table that you're on, assess how your opponents are playing in different situations. By the time you get to the middle stage, you should know which players are moving in which situations, which players are liable to call you and which ones are not.

You also know that the worst play that you can ever make is to bluff at a bad player. Bad players will not lay down a hand, even in a tournament. They don't know any better. If you're going to run a bluff, you should run it at a good player because he's not afraid to lay down a hand. In the first round when the blinds are relatively small, there may be some occasions when you can bluff, but mostly, you're just waiting for a good hand and the right opening to try to trap your opponents. Usually, it is the weaker players that you're waiting to trap, not the strong ones — the strong ones are waiting to do exactly the same thing to you!

SEMI-AGGRESSIVENESS

Tom explains what we mean by becoming semi-aggressive and opening up, stepping up your action a notch or two: "In this middle stage, around the fourth or fifth level, the big blinds are about $200. At this point, players are beginning to accumulate chips and about one-half of the field has been eliminated. Say that you have inched up the size of your stack from your original $2,000 in chips to $2,500 and you now have a sub-standard stack. You can't just sit there and play a super-conservative game, because the blinds are becoming too big. So, you have to open up your game a bit, take a few more risks."

PICKING YOUR SPOTS

Taking a few more risks means picking spots when you can be the aggressor, when you can be the first one in the pot — when you can do the pushing, not the calling. For example, if you're in a middle position, you might raise it up with the A♦ 10♦ or the K♣ J♣, whereas you may have passed with those hands earlier. Of course, if you get too much action, you have to pass. You might do the same types of things if you have doubled or tripled up and have one of the bigger stacks at the table, when everybody else is just hanging on.

PLAYING A SHORT STACK

However, you don't want to open up too much if you're half-stacked, because you are more likely to get called or played with. You want to wait for a big pair or A-K, or play aggressively only in the last two seats.

Short-stacked or not, if nobody has entered the pot and you're two spots away from the button, you're not going to throw away the A♦ 10♦. If you get raised, you can throw away your hand without committing all of your chips to it. Short-stacked, I am going to move in all of my chips from fifth position on back with this type of hand, if I have to — or at least put in enough chips to become committed to the pot. You're far less likely to get away from a hand short-stacked than if you have a bigger stack.

The point is that you have to take more risks with a short stack. You can't just wait around for aces or A-K because you don't get them often enough. You don't need to have a giant hand to start making some moves. Just be sure that in these situations, you are the aggressor: You are not reacting to your opponents, *they* are reacting to you.

The only time that this strategy doesn't run true is when you're playing against super-aggressive players who are sitting behind you, because they are liable to chop you off quickly. If you're playing with normal players, decent players, this is a very good strategy. But if you have a Stu Ungar type sitting behind you with a lot of chips, it doesn't work that well.

At this middle stage, you probably will see more two or three-way pots, whereas in the earlier stages there were a lot more multiway pots. There isn't nearly as much limping from the second round onward. The people who were playing any two suited cards in the earlier rounds are usually out of the tournament by now.

LATE STAGE

At different stages in the tournament, you change your style of play from being aggressive to playing semi-aggressively to playing more passively. In the early stage, you play solid poker. In the middle stage, you can play semi-aggressively, opening up your play in the right spots. Then in the late stage, when it gets to three or four tables, you play passively for a while. At a full table, you are still playing ring-game strategy. You want other players to knock each other out so that you can get to the final table.

Then you get to the "move" period when you're three or four out of the money. This is when you play aggressive poker so that you can accumulate chips to be competitive at the money table. When it gets down to two from the money, you can play very aggressively. However, if you're a couple of places out of the money with a short stack, you have a lot less maneuverability. You can't get too far out of line because somebody is going to look you up, hoping to bust you. At this stage, aggressive players like Men Nguyen accumulate a lot chips by constantly keeping the heat on their opponents.

With a medium or slightly above average stack, your opponents won't want to mess with you unless they have a real hand because it always takes greater strength to call a raise than to make a raise. In tournaments, you have to be very careful about the hands that you call raises with.

BETTING YOURSELF OUT OF A POT

Tom discusses the danger of playing a drawing hand and betting yourself out of a pot: "In pot-limit and no-limit tournaments and ring games, there are times when you might aggressively bet a drawing hand because you think that you have a reasonable expectation of winning the pot. But there are other times when you are far better off to just take a free card, especially when you are playing against tricky and aggressive players who do a lot of check-raising.

For example, suppose you have slipped into the pot from late position with:

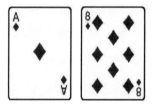

The flop comes:

There are three people in front of you in the pot, and two of them are tricky and aggressive. With this flop, you often would take a card off if somebody bets because you have an overcard working and the nut flush draw. But what if nobody bets on the flop? Against aggressive and tricky opponents, it is usually correct to also check and take the free card.

If you place a bet, especially if you make a pot-size bet, if somebody comes over the top of you with a maximum reraise, you will have to jeopardize too many of your chips to take the draw ... unless either one of you is so short-stacked that you decide to go with the hand. You are better off in taking the free card and trying to hit your draw for nothing.

Now, let's look at a different scenario. You have the same A♦ 8♦ and the flop is the same, but you're up against only one opponent. Say that you have made a positional raise before the flop, the big blind called you, and now you are head-up. If he checks to you on the flop, you can bet the hand. Or say that, in addition to the big blind, there is one limper in the pot. They both are somewhat passive players. If they both check to you on the flop, then you can bet.

Any time that you think a bet will win the pot for you, go ahead and bet. Since a king is on the board, they may put you on a pair of kings rather than a flush draw. If neither of them has a king, it would be difficult for them to call your button bet. If one of them calls you with a little king (a K-7, for example), you can always check on the turn (if you have no improvement) and wait for the river card to try to make your hand.

Of course, you could also make a second bet on the turn card if you think that it will win the pot for you, but that is a judgment call based on your knowledge of your opponents. There is always the danger that you could have made your hand cheaply, whereas you might get blown off the pot if you take an aggressive posture.

Remember than in pot-limit or no-limit, players can distort the size of the pot by putting in a significant bet, raise, or reraise. With a hand that you probably will make only one in three times, you will be paying too high a price if you have to put in a large amount of money to draw to it. This is why you have to be very selective when you have a drawing hand. Some players play drawing hands too aggressively, rather than kicking back and playing them more passively.

Another situation of this type is when you flop bottom two pair and are first to act. Suppose you are in the blind with 8-7, and the flop comes J-8-7. Bottom two pair can be a dangerous hand. Say that you lead at the pot against several players and one of them comes over the top of you with a huge raise. There could be a straight out there, a set, or top two pair. In this scenario, it is better to check from the front and see what happens, rather than making a major commitment to the pot. If you had the same bottom two pair in last position, you might put in a bet if it is checked to you, taking the risk of being check raised.

Now, say that you are in late position in an unraised pot with only two other people, and you have flopped bottom two pair. One of your opponents, a known aggressive player who will represent hands that he doesn't have, bets in front of you. In this case, I might come over the top of him to protect my two pair. Again, it all goes back to playing the players and the situation.

Be leery of betting yourself off a hand that has some potential. If you can get a free card that may make the hand for you, the superior strategy often is to take the free card. When you make a risky bet, you may open it up for someone to come over the top of you and force you to fold when you could have had a free card, possibly have made your hand, and then have gotten some action on it."

THE LAST THREE TABLES

From the minute that I sit down in a tournament, my goal is to make it to the top three payoff spots. It is never my goal to just get my money back. Actually, I'm only thinking of winning, but I will be satisfied to place in the top three because that's where the money is. But first, I have to move up from the third table to the final table.

Tom talks about strategy at the final three tables. "By now, you know your opponents. Your strategy is based on that knowledge and your chip count. The more chips you have, the more options and weapons you have. If you are one of the shorter stacks, you know that you will be somewhat on the defensive; you don't have enough chips to intimidate your opponents. The bigger stacks are looking to bust you, and are sometimes willing to gamble with a slightly more marginal hand in order to beat you. You are the bulls eye to them.

If you have an average stack or a big stack, it's a different ball game. An opponent has to have a hand to commit against you, unless he is extremely short-stacked and decides to take a stand, or unless he has a big stack and is willing to mix it up with anybody because he has a huge lead."

PLAYING A BIG STACK

When the top players have a lot of chips at the last three tables, they are not going to say, "Well, I'm going to take a chance to bust this guy." The top players are not going to jeopardize their chips on a weaker hand. They want to get to the top three positions, so why should they give anybody a chance to double up at their expense? Top players will have a playable hand when they come into a pot, or they're going to be the aggressor.

The old proverb in hold'em is, "A bettor be or a raiser be; a caller never be." This is a very good guideline for this stage of play. If you're betting a pot, you could have the worst hand or the best hand, but you always have the chance to win because you bet. If you're calling, you have only one option: "Maybe I have this guy beaten."

The only time that you should be a caller past the flop in pot-limit or no-limit hold'em is when you are setting up an opponent, when you are laying a trap. For example, at the final table at the WSOP in 1993, it was down to three-handed with John Bonetti, Jim Bechtel, and Glenn Cozen. Bechtel had two sixes and Bonetti held an A-K. A lot of players in Bechtel's spot would have raised with the sixes, but Bechtel didn't. He played the hand to either catch a six or to throw it away. He knew that Bonetti had a big hand and that if he caught a six, he could trap Bonetti for a lot of money. Of course, he caught the six on the flop.

But the point is that Bechtel played the hand correctly, whereas a lesser player would either have moved in with the hand or would have thrown it away.

THE FINAL TABLE

Now it's nitty-gritty time, the time when you can win the tournament. To start with, you're playing in a full ring of nine players. In nine-handed play, you still want to try to play top hand all of the time. Of course, top hand doesn't have to be two aces; it could be two fives in certain situations. You play the best hand, whatever that best hand may be.

You will be playing basic strategy, except that you can sometimes pick up pots because the blinds are so big at this stage. However, you have to be very careful about when you try to do it. If you're the type of player who raises every time it's passed to you on the button, whether you have a hand or you don't, somebody is eventually going to chop you off.

STEAL SITUATIONS

If you're going to try to steal a pot, you don't always need to be on the button. You can steal from in front of the button or two spots away from the button. I've even done it from the first seat. If you're raising from the first seat into eight other players, they're going to give you a lot of credit, especially if you have an image. Your opponents will have to have a pretty strong hand to call you, so you'll see them mucking hands such as A-J, A-Q, and K-Q suited.

If I have been raised by a front position player, I might not necessarily muck my hand; it depends on what I know about his play. This is where that sixth sense that we've talked about comes into play, your feel for what's going on in the mind of the raiser, whether he is capable of making a semi-bluff raise from up front. Most players are not capable of raising with a hand such as 9♥ 8♥, but a few of them are.

BREAKING OTHER PLAYERS

At the final table, remember that you don't have to break everybody at the table. Wait and let them break each other. Tom admits to getting to the last table in good chip position when he first started playing tournaments and, seeing that everybody was playing passively, taking it upon himself to bust people out of the tournament. I think that we've probably all done that early in our careers. What often happens is that you bust several people out, then get to the final three, and finish in third place.

Tom explains that "I didn't slow down enough. I took risks against the short stacks, but of course, once you're in the top three, nobody is short-stacked. Then I got sawed off. I may have been better off by not knocking out as many people, by being a tad more selective or a tad less aggressive, by playing fewer hands.

You see, you usually get a lot of respect by playing aggressively in short-handed play, but because I had been playing a ton of hands before the game got short-handed, my image had changed. My opponents didn't give me as much respect as they ordinarily would have given me, especially since they had seen me play a weak hand and bust out a player with it. Now they were more willing to mix it up with me, to go after me. So, it sometimes can work against you if your table image has changed during your play at the final table."

THE FINAL FIVE

Now suppose it's down to five players. At this point, I'm going to get a little more aggressive. Of course, how aggressive I become depends on how many chips I have. If you have the command position in chips, people are always worried about messing with you in a pot because they know that you can break them. You can look around the table and see who is trying to outlast the others.

For example, I was playing four-handed in a $500 tournament at the High Sierra and saw that two of the short stacks were trying to outlast each other just to survive and make it to the bigger money. They were playing what Tom calls "not to lose." I took advantage of them like Grant going through Richmond — and you can do the same thing in a similar situation. You just keep chipping away at them, and since the blinds are so high, you're *really* chipping away because it's so expensive to play at that level.

PLAYING A SHORT STACK

If you're one of the short stacks when it gets down to five-or-so players, you have to find a hand that you like and just go with it. The main thing that you cannot do is to let yourself get so short that the next time you have to post a blind, it will eat up all of your chips. Then, even if you double up, all you will have left is what you had before you were forced to post the blinds. You always have to make your move *before* you get so short stacked that doubling up won't help you. This might mean moving in with virtually nothing.

I once played a tournament in which I had lost a couple of big pots. We were down to seven-handed play, the antes were $300, and the blinds were $1,000-$2,000. I had $8,000 in chips and it was costing me $5,100 a round to play. In the big blind, I held a 9-2 offsuit. The action was passed all the way around to the button, who held an A-J. He raised and moved me all-in. My only hope in playing the hand was that I had live cards against an ace or a king because with five cards to come, I was only a 2-to-1 dog with any two live cards. I won the hand, and pretty soon, I had $70,000 in chips.

The key idea in this example is that I didn't let myself get anteed and blinded down to the point that doubling up wouldn't have helped me. I'm not suggesting that you make this type of play, of course, and if you do, you have to know that the guy on the button will raise without having a pair in his hand. If he's the type of player who only raises with paris, you cannot make the call. In this situation (you are in the big blind), the only two raisers that you can call are the button and the little blind; you cannot call from a front position, for example.

You should always know *what* you are doing in a specific situation and *why* you are doing it. In this case, I made the call to try to avoid getting so short-chipped that even doubling up couldn't pull me out of the hole.

PLAYING HEAD-UP

Any time that you are head-up with an opponent who has a 3-to-1 chip lead over you, remember that you are still only two all-in hands away from winning the tournament. Sometimes when you're playing head-up, you can move into a "zone," something like the great marathon runners talk about.

For example, at the Diamond Jim Brady no-limit hold'em tournament in 1991, I had $120,000 and Tuna Lund had $360,000. I was chipping away at him, meaning that I was winning every pot from him by being super-aggressive. In fact, I won fourteen out of fifteen hands, a little bit here and a little bit there. When it came to the point that he was only 2-to-1 in chips against me, Tuna asked if I wanted to make a deal. I said no, and we continued to play. I had been chipping away at him so badly that I knew he was going to run a bluff on me. It had gotten to the stage where he had to try to take the aggressive position away from me.

Then a hand came up when a J-9-4 came on the flop. I have been known to play the J-9, but this time I only had a nine. Tuna bet the flop and I raised him just a little bit. Then off came a three. He took the lead with a $40,000 bet, and I thought to myself, "I know I've got him, even though I only have second pair."

I called the $40,000, and thought that if neither a king nor an ace came on the river, he was going to bluff the pot.

The board paired threes on the end, which was perfect for my hand. Tuna bet $50,000 and I called. "Before you turn your hand over," I told him, "let me tell you what you have. You have a Q-10 offsuit." He turned his hand over and there it was, the Q-10. Just as I thought, he had picked up a draw to the J-9, and I predicted that if he didn't hit it, he would bluff at me on the river. Suddenly, I had the lead in the tournament. A few hands later, I raised with two tens, he moved all-in with two eights, and it was all over.

The year before that at the Diamond Jim Brady tournament, Mansour Matloubi and I got head-up. I had the J♥ 7♥ in my hand and he had two hearts in his hand. The board came with two hearts and a seven. I led at the pot and he called. On fourth street a rag came, he checked to me, I bet, and he called.

On the end, there were three overcards to the seven on the board. Mansour had not run a bluff for five hours of play at the final table, and he put his last $120,000 in on the river. I beat him into the pot with fourth-best pair. He said, "You've got me. I'm bluffing."

THE ZONE

Head-up is a whole different ball game. You can make these types of moves based on your observation, your feel for the game, and your opponents. When you're in your zone, your opponent recognizes that and he has to make a move to get you out of your cycle. To this day, Mansour laughs about my calling him with those two sevens, saying that it was the greatest play he's ever seen in hold'em. Of course, the call wouldn't have busted me, but that didn't enter into my decision. I was in the zone, and when you're there, you have "balls of iron," you *know* when you have the best hand.

Tom observed that "You have to have the courage of your convictions in spots like this, when you have a dead read on your opponent. Many times, a player will have the same read, but won't have the courage to act on his convictions. He takes the easy way out and mucks his hand."

The third time that I won the Diamond Jim Brady, I was at the final table with Eskimo Clark, Hal Kant, and

Bobby Hoff, who was short-stacked. I brought it in, Kant folded, Eskimo raised it, and Bobby moved in his short stack. I thought, "Well, I know that Eskimo has some kind of a king-hand, judging from the way he has been raising four-handed. I have A-J here and I have a lot of chips, so I'm going to move over the top of Bobby and shut Eskimo out to get head-up with Bobby."

And that's exactly the move that I made. Eskimo folded his K-Q, and Bobby and I ended up splitting the pot since we both had an A-J. But the board came K-Q and to this day, Eskimo still talks about having had the best hand. But before the flop, he didn't have top hand and I shut him out so that he couldn't win the pot. These are the types of plays that come with experience and from the feel that you develop for certain situations.

In head-up play, you are no longer concerned about chip count and you don't need as strong a starting hand to get involved with. Any ace is super-powerful. Pocket pairs, eights and higher, also are strong, but small pocket pairs, the deuces through the sevens, are not nearly as strong as they are in other head-up situations because players will call you with hands like J-10 and 9-8 because they are only 11-to-10 dogs. You might play the lower pairs, but you shouldn't commit all your money with them before the flop. If your opponent has two paints in his hand, he will probably call a raise. The all-powerful card in head-up play is the ace.

"MOVE" TIMES IN TOURNAMENTS

There are certain "move" periods in tournaments. One of them is when you're one table away from the pay table. At the WSOP, which pays the final three tables, the move period is at the fourth table. Actually, it is two players away from the third table, when everybody is trying to survive to get into the money. You can pick up a mountain of chips at this time, and that's when top players can amass so many chips by capitalizing on the situation.

Another move time is when it's down to five players at the final table. All of the money is in the last three spots, so everybody is trying to get into at least third place. You have to know *how* to move and *when* to execute against which players.

Tom talks about this in *Championship Tournament Poker*, where he says that you have to capitalize on your opponents' tight play. If you're willing to take a few extra risks, knowing that you might bust out and miss the big money, you have a chance at a massive reward, because all of the money is piled on the top three spots. You have to take selective risks in the right spots.

GETTING INTO THE MONEY

I would hate to tell you how many times I have finished one out of the money because I was trying to win the tournament instead of getting into the money. At the WSOP in 1996, for example, we were down to twenty-nine players and I had about $70,000 in chips. Akron John, who is a very aggressive player, was at my table. I was on the button, John was two seats to my right, and Huck Seed (who went on to win it) was sitting between us.

Any time the action got around to the last five players, John seemed to raise the pot and usually didn't need a hand to do it, either. He brought it in for something between $6,000 and $8,000. I looked down at my hand and found two tens, so I raised him $27,000. I knew that he would throw away his hand and I would win all of those big antes and the blinds. But Men Nguyen was sitting in the little blind behind me holding two red aces and came back over the top, so both Akron John and I threw away our hands.

A little later, I had built my stack back up to $50,000 when a hand came up in which John brought it in for $8,000, Huck Seed called, and I moved all in with A♦ Q♦. I knew that I had both of them beaten and that they would throw away their hands. Winning it right there would get my stack up to around $80,000. But again, Men was sitting behind me with two aces in the little blind, and I was knocked out of the tournament.

The point is that there was no reason why I couldn't have gotten into the money and been able to come back for the third day of play. But I was trying to get some chips by situational play, trying to win the tournament. Although they didn't work out, I believe that both plays were correct. There were only two people behind me and both times, Men held aces. (Earlier, he had broken Alex Brenes with two aces when Alex held two kings.)

All of the great players like Johnny Chan, Eric Seidel, and Jim Bechtel make moves at the right time. Dan Harrington is another great player who knows how to do this. For years, he was called "Action Dan" because he gave *no* action; he was the tightest player in the world.

But he has developed a tournament strategy in which he plays some strange cards and picks up a lot of pots in the right places.

The point is that there is a basic tournament formula or strategy, but then you have to adjust it for your own cubicle, for the way that you play your cards. For example, I never had played in a seven-card stud tournament until one year when Phil Hellmuth (who was backing me at the time) wanted me to play a stud satellite. So, I played in the $5,000 satellite, won a seat in the tournament, and finished in fourth place. From then on, I had to play all of the stud tournaments and went on to win a first, two seconds, two thirds, and a fourth in the first dozen tournaments that I ever played by simply adapting the tournament style of play that I had used in other events, a style that is completely different from side games.

You see, no matter what the game is, when you hit the final table, the *real* game is still tournament poker.

T.J. at the table

5

HOW TO WIN NO-LIMIT HOLD'EM TOURNAMENTS

From 1981 until 1992, I played no-limit hold'em in Dallas from noon until 5:00 p.m. every Monday through Friday, and from 7:00 p.m. to midnight or later five days a week. On Sundays, I drove to Shreveport to play pot-limit hold'em. I was putting in sixty hours a week, and sometimes eighty, playing no-limit and pot-limit poker during these eleven years. Players used to come from all over the nation to play in our game at a place that we will call The Big Texan's. His house had the best food and the cleanest environment you could ask for, and it was a safe game, too.

All the road gamblers came to play in the game — Willie Struthers, Berry Johnston and Steve Melvin drove in from Oklahoma City, Garland Walters came in from Kentucky, Gene Fisher from El Paso, Bobby Baldwin, Buddy Williams, all the best players. That game was a great training ground in no-limit hold'em. Tom told me, "I lost about $15,000 playing no-limit hold'em in that game, but I won $40,000 at pot-limit Omaha. Until then,

I thought I was a no-limit hold'em player — boy, did I learn a few lessons! People that I'd never heard of before were some of the best players that I had ever seen."

The Big Texan was a big whale of a man and he ran the best game in Dallas. But he was one of the most disliked men there, too. I'm a very calm person, but there were three times in those 11 years when I almost stood up and let him have it. I didn't because I knew that this was a game in which I could make a lot of money and I wasn't going to get shut out of it. One night we were playing no-limit hold'em and I raised the pot $200 with A-Q suited. The Big Texan called it. It got around to Walter Jones, and he put in his last $400. This was a legal raise because the raise in no-limit hold'em has to be double the amount of the original raise. I decided I was going to shut the Big Texan out of the pot so I came back over the top with $2,000 to get head-up with Jones. "That's not a raise," the Big Texan said.

"The hell if it's not," I answered. "It's as legal as it can be." Everybody at the table was agreeing with me, when the Big Texan just reached over and slapped me on the hand. Well, I reared up and I was really going to let him have it because I never cared for him one iota anyway. But I thought better of it because I needed that game; it paid all my expenses for the year. Of course, the raise stood and he threw his hand away. He told me later that if I had hit him, he would've gone for his gun. "Buddy," I said, "if I had hit you, you'd never have had a chance to get that gun out."

The Big Texan was always afraid that the money would leave Dallas. When I was still just dating my wife Joy, he called her and said, "How come you let T. J. go out to those tournaments? Don't you know that he could lose all his money in those things?" He's the same one that said he was going to drop the latch on me after I'd won twelve times in a row in his game. "You're beating these boys too bad," he said, "and I don't want that money going back to Louisiana. But if you'll let me have half of your play, you can keep on playing here."

So for the next eleven games, the Big Texan was in on my action and we won all eleven times. On the twelfth night, he said, "I'm out today." That was just like a bell going off in my head; I knew that something was going to go down in the game that day. There were a few strangers from Oklahoma in the game that I'd never seen before. So I just bought in for $500 instead of the usual $1,000, played for about an hour, and left. And the Big Texan never came in with me again.

There were a ton of good players in Dallas. In fact, if you could beat the Dallas game, you could beat any game, including the World Series of Poker. You see, the World Series is a conglomeration of local champions. There's Joe Blow from Iowa who's the champion in his game at home; hundreds of local champions like him come to Vegas to play the World Series. But it's like the difference in going from playing high school football to college football: It's a big step up. And then going from college to pro football is the next big step.

It's not a question of whether these players can play poker — they just can't play it on the level that some of the top players can. It's similar to Tiger Woods. There are a lot of great golfers out there right now, but Tiger Woods is *the* golfer, the one with the most talent. There is a lot of skill difference among poker pros, too. The top pros have a higher skill level that they have developed over a long period of time.

I started playing the tournaments in 1978. When the World Series was going on, the poker game in Dallas would shut down. The same thing happened during Amarillo Slim's Super Bowl of Poker and the Stardust's Stairway to the Stars because a lot of Dallas players entered these tournaments. As the result, I became well versed in tournament play and have won the championship event in all of them except for the World Series, where I placed second to Bill Smith in 1985.

Sometimes, you'll see a player win one tournament here, another one there. And it's true that anybody can win a tournament; that's the beauty of poker. You can go on a rush in the right spot and win it; however, it's less likely to happen in no-limit and pot-limit than it is in other games because the skill level is so much higher. Sometimes, in a one-day tournament, a weaker player will slip through the cracks, but in the four-day big one at the World Series, it's far less likely to happen. That's because no-limit hold'em is the Cadillac of poker—there are more moves you can make and more traps that you have to avoid than in any other game. When you get down to the end in most no-limit tournaments, even the $500 buy-in ones, most of the players at the final table are recognizable. That is not the case in the limit games.

So, winning one tournament doesn't make you a good player—it's winning a whole series of tournaments that establishes you as a top player.

NO-LIMIT HOLD'EM STYLE

People used to ask me, "Why do you do well in tournaments?" I told them that in my broke days when I was traveling two hundred miles from Shreveport to play in Dallas with just one buy-in, I got used to playing a short stack — I couldn't go to my pocket for more. In tournaments, you can't go to your pocket, unless it's a rebuy tournament.

So, I developed a style of play in which I learned to protect my chips and, at the same time, build them, not taking any chances. In no-limit, the more chances you take, the more chances you have of getting busted because all of your money can go in one bet. You learn survival. That's the thing you have to learn to win tournaments.

The thing that makes it so hard to play with just one buy-in or a short stack in no-limit hold'em ring games is that no-limit is a game designed for people who have a lot of money in front of them. To play correctly in a side game, you always want to have enough money in front of you, as much or more than any other player on the table, because that one hand might come up in which you could bust them. It's a terrible thing to have $500 while your opponent has $5,000, because if you win a pot from that man, all you can win is $500.

Chips speak in no-limit. This is one reason why I maintain that the game doesn't really start in a no-limit tournament until the antes go into effect at the second $100-$200 level. You have to survive until you hit that point.

PLAYING STYLE

In the first few rounds of a tournament, people usually try to play their best games, but over a long period of time, they're going to play their regular game. You have to be very careful and know how the player is playing at any particular time in the game. Some players come out of the shoot firing, and never change their style. They play the same from start to finish. A player like Mel Weiner, for example, will play aggressively early and if he happens to get some chips, then he slows down.

Hamid Dastmalchi is a great player, and early in his career I saw him go into a shell at the final table in two separate tournaments. His opponents just flat worked him over while he was in his shell and he wound up losing both times. He may have been just waiting for a big hand, or he might have been over protecting his lead. Tom says that some players in that situation aren't playing to *win*, they're playing *not* to lose.

So, the year that he won the World Series, I took Hamid outside and talked to him during a break. I said, "Look, Hamid, I'm out of the tournament, but if you're going to win it, you had better play your style. Don't do what you did the last time." Then a hand came up at the final table between him and Jack Keller. Hamid raised the pot with A-K and Jack came back over the top of him. Then Hamid moved all in and Jack called him with almost all of his chips.

Hamid won the hand with either an ace or a king. Although I thought that they both played the hand poorly, at least Hamid was playing more of his aggressive style.

CLOUTIER & MCEVOY • CARDOZA PUBLISHING

OBSERVATION

Observation is very important in pot-limit hold'em, but it's even more crucial in no-limit hold'em. You see, no-limit hold'em is the only game in which you can continually win pots without a hand. In other games, you have to show down a hand to win, but you can win money in no-limit just by seizing situations. Now, you can't think that you can do this all the time or you're going to get chopped off. You have to be smart enough to pick your situations and the right time.

LOOKING AT YOUR HAND

I always look at my hand quickly. If you look at your hand before the action comes to you, you can see whether anything is going on behind you. If you wait until the action gets to you to look at your hand, you will miss a lot of things. Look at your hand as soon as you get both of your cards so that you can observe the things that other players are doing when they get their cards:

• Little twitches they make when they have a hand
• Whether they slip their cards back under their chips
• Whether they are loading up, getting their chips ready to bet.

You often will be able to tell whether a player is going to play the pot. This alone will save you a lot of money because if you know that somebody behind you will either call or raise the pot, you can throw away a marginal hand that you might have called with and it won't cost you any chips or money.

121

TIMING IS EVERYTHING

Timing is everything in no-limit hold'em. It's not the hands that you play, it's *when* you play them, and who you're playing against. You might have 7-2—and I'm not telling you to play this hand—but it might be *time* to play 7-2.

A hand came up once in Dallas when I was playing against all the top players around and was running good. I was on the button looking down at this:

There were five limpers in front of me. "I'm gonna' steal this pot," I said to myself, and put in a $400 raise. Much to my dismay, three of them called me. But the flop came 7-7-2. Now, how could they have put me on a hand like that?! This isn't something that you want to do very often, of course ... it was just a matter of timing.

Although I try to stay away from all draws in tournaments, back in 1985 a hand came up when I was playing against Bones Berland. It was the type of year that when I played a pot, I won it.

I was on the button with this:

There were two or three limpers in front of me who were somewhat weak. I thought that I'd just pick up the pot right then and pick up the antes for a few free rounds. I was sitting there with about $40,000 in chips and raised the pot $1,000. Bones called me.

The flop came 4-5-7 with two hearts. Bones made a bet at the pot and I raised him. He was holding two tens and called with all of his money. Of course, I busted him on the hand — It was just a matter of timing.

When I told Tom this story, he mentioned that if Berland had come in with a raise, I would have had to muck my hand, but he didn't and I was able to play off of his mistake. Poker is a game of mistakes. You cannot win in a poker game if everybody in the game plays perfectly. If the cards break even in a no-limit poker game, Tom and I figure to win. Any player in an average game figures to win if his skill level is superior.

There isn't a player alive who doesn't make mistakes — nobody is good enough to be mistake free — but those who make fewer mistakes will win the money. This is why you have to continue to learn all the time you're playing. I've been playing for a lot of years, and I learn something new every day— mostly, how other players play a hand.

MAKING MISTAKES

A good player doesn't hope to get a 60-40 break in the cards. If the cards break even, a good player will win the money at all times because he's going to make fewer mistakes than a bad player will make.

What does poker break down to in the long run?

Most of the money you make comes from somebody's mistakes. Good players also make mistakes, but they make fewer of them.

Tom told me a story about a simple mistake that he made in a small tournament at Crystal Park in California. "My mistake was that I didn't call in the big blind with the 6♠ 3♠ against the chip leader, who had been playing every hand. Now, you wouldn't think that 6♠ 3♠ would be a hand that you could make a mistake with by folding, but it was a mistake.

I had one-half of my chips in the pot, and would have to put in two of my three remaining chips on the very next hand. The circumstances made it a mistake to fold the 6-3, not because it figured to be the best starting hand, but because I already had half of my money in the pot and should have played the two suited cards.

If I didn't figure the raiser to be holding a pair, the worst off I could have been was a 2-to-1 underdog. The chip leader raised the next hand when I had the Q♣ 2♣ in the small blind, and I put in my last chip. He was holding two queens, and busted me out of the tournament."

One of the biggest mistake that people make in no-limit hold'em is raising the pot with a medium pair from early position, leaving themselves open to a reraise. If a good player knows that Player A is the type of player that raises with these types of hands, sooner or later he's going to pop him with nothing and make Player A lay down his hand. If you call the raise with a medium pair from up front, then you're compounding your mistake. Ninety-nine percent of the time, you should just throw that medium pair away because it simply cannot stand a reraise.

You have to be very selective about the hands that

you raise with. For example, an A-K or A-Q is a very sensible hand to raise with from around back, but it's a piece of cheese to raise with from up front, especially if someone pops you — The A-K is called "Walking Back to Houston" because so many of the road gamblers got broke with the hand, even lost their cars betting with it, and (figuratively speaking) had to "walk" two hundred miles back to Houston from Dallas.

Never set your sights on one player in the ring. A lot of people make the mistake of thinking that, because a guy's getting way out of line, they're going to chop him off. But if you think that way, you can get caught in the middle, especially when you're playing in a full game. Shoot at one player when you're only playing one player. Don't make the mistake of saying to yourself, "Well, I'm a better player than this guy, and he's going to make a mistake, and I'm just gong to gobble him up."

Invariably, you will be caught in the middle and somebody behind you will knock you off.

BUILDING AND PROTECTING YOUR CHIPS

In tournaments, you have to build your chips ... but you also have to protect your chips. Therefore, you have to be very, very careful, especially in the early rounds while the tables are still full. Suppose that you have the $1,000 that you started with and you look around and see one player with $5,000, another one with $8,000. That should not affect your play one iota. You can't control *their* stacks, you can only control *your own* stack.

Because somebody has chips early in the tournament

doesn't mean a thing. His rush may be over by the time it gets down to the nitty-gritty, something that happens most of the time. Many times, the early chip leaders are not *good* players — they're *lucky* players who have been playing a lot of pots. Even though they have the chip lead, they will make enough mistakes in the later stages that their stacks will dwindle because they continue to play too many hands.

You have to be selective in the hands that you play in no-limit hold'em. In tournaments, the one overriding factor that you always have to consider is, "I must survive to have a chance to win." You have to think about that all of the time. This is why I play a conservative game early. I don't worry about how many chips I have early in the tournament; I'm a plodder. I know that the opportunities will come. My ultimate scenario is that at the end of every break, I have more chips than I had at the previous break.

In the late rounds, protecting your chips is also important. Tom told me the story of a player who got to the final table in second chip position. She was holding an A-blank in 10-handed play when she decided to make a play at the only player at the table who could have busted her, a guy who had been playing every hand. The flop came with two face cards and she bluffed off all of her money against the other big stack, who called her bluff with second pair. Who made the bigger mistake—the guy who had been playing every hand, or the one who decided to take after him ten-handed?

She was more out of line because she had chips to protect. Also, she didn't raise him enough to prevent him from calling. When she raised, she needed to have showered down on him with the raise.

Another mistake that was made in the play of this hand was going up against another big stack. When you're in this type of situation, you want to attack the small stacks and stay clear of the other big stacks when you don't hold the nuts, because they are the ones that can really hurt you. You want to play against the big stacks when you have a premium hand because you want to double through them; but with less than a premium hand, you don't want to mess with them.

When the action gets down to between four and two tables, Tom likes to walk around and see where he stands in the tournament. "It's not that I'm fearful of their stacks, I just want to make sure where I stand when I'm x-number of seats out of the money, and who looks as though they're close to going out," he said. "Then I can determine my best strategy." I don't believe that you should play in a tournament with any other idea than to win it. If winning is your goal at all times, you're going to play better, play aggressively when you have to, and even play passively in certain spots.

TOURNAMENT STRUCTURE

The difference between pot-limit and no-limit tournaments is that in no-limit, an ante goes in when you hit the second level of the $100-$200 blinds. That is, during the first level of $100-$200 blinds, there is no ante; but when it goes to the second level of $100-$200 blinds (usually about the fourth or fifth round of play), the ante goes into effect, beginning at $25.

This is the way it's done at the World Series of Poker

and at all other major tournaments.

In pot-limit, there is never an ante, so it is always cheaper to play a hand in a pot-limit tournament than it is to play a hand in no-limit. When you get up into the $100-$200 blinds in no-limit, you're also anteing $25 a hand, so it's costing you $525 a round to play. But I have always maintained that the *main* difference between pot-limit and no-limit tournament play is that you can play weaker hands in pot-limit than you can in no-limit.

TYPES OF HANDS TO START WITH IN EARLY POSITION

In the first round of the World Series, as well as in the first round of the smaller buy-in events at the WSOP, a pair of kings is not a big enough hand to get broke with. The only hand that is big enough to get broke with before the flop is two aces.

In the early positions, you only want to play Ace-King or better. When I say A-K or better, I'm not talking about playing the small pairs, although you might limp with a pair of eights or better. If I am holding A-Q (suited or unsuited) *or worse* in the first four or five seats, I don't want to put even a dime in the pot during the first few levels in a full nine or ten-handed game. Always treat being suited as a little added luxury, a factor that should not change your decision to play a hand that you ordinarily would not play. Your hand is still A-Q — being suited is just an added plus. The value of the hand is in its ranks, not in its being suited.

You cannot stand a good raise with the A-Q from an early position in the opening rounds. If you catch either the ace or the queen, you are put into a quandary about what to do next if someone bets at you. Do you throw it away, do you raise, or do you call? Why put yourself in that situation?

Tom says that he tries to avoid having to make any tricky decisions. He would rather come in with any pair than an A-Q in those first four spots because a small-to-medium pair plays very easily after the flop — No set, no bet. The A-Q or A-J, however, require a lot of finesse and judgment to play after the flop if you get any action.

PLAYING THE SMALL PAIRS

I do not play baby pairs, but I might just flat call with a pair of eights or better from early position, hoping that I don't get raised. If I do get raised, I just throw them away, since I only have a minimum amount in the pot. One big tournament winner that I know likes to come in with a raise before the flop with little pairs, hoping that he will flop a set that nobody will put him on, and hoping that he won't get blown off the hand by a big raise behind him. It's a risk that he's willing to take. Just remember that you cannot handle any heat with the small pairs before the flop.

Tom doesn't mind limping in with the small pairs or bringing them in for a small raise. He will stand a small raise and try to catch a set on the flop. Say that he brings it in for $50 and someone makes it $150 or $200. If he has $5,000 or more chips in front of him, he might call the raise, but will give no further action on the flop unless he flops the set. I very seldom do that.

I want to take out a player, just like everyone else

does, but if I'm going to play a small pair, I don't want to play it against only one opponent; I want to play it in a multiway pot. Then if I make a set, I might really make some money on the hand. I don't understand why a person would play small pairs head-up, when they know that they are a dog to start with. The time to play the small pairs is when you are in late position or when you are in a short-handed game.

PLAYING THE ACE-KING

More tournaments are won or lost with Ace-King against a big pair than any other hand. You might be up against two queens, flop an ace or a king, and win the pot, although the queens are an 11-to-10 favorite if you play 10,000 hands. But if you are running unlucky, it seems like somebody always catches up on the last two cards. To win a no-limit tournament, you have to win with A-K and you have to beat A-K. You may not win or lose with them on the final hand, but it usually will be the deciding hand, the one that wins or loses the most chips for you. It's the biggest decision-hand in a tournament.

Early in the tournament, I treat A-K very softly. I might make a raise with it, but I'm not going to lose any money to it if I don't flop pretty good to it. If someone raises from the front when I'm holding A-K in the back, the way that I handle it largely depends on the player who makes the raise. There are times when I will just flat call the raise. There are times when I will try to win the money right then by reraising. And there are times when I will simply throw the hand away. It all depends on what I know about my opponent, how he's playing that day.

The second year that Johnny Chan won the World Series, when it was down to two tables, he played twelve times in 11-to-10 situations, either a big pair against two overcards or vice-versa — and he won all twelve times, which gave him chips for the final table. In his last hand against Frank Henderson, a similar situation came up. Johnny made a raise before the flop with A-9 and Henderson moved all-in. A nine came at the river to beat Henderson, who held pocket fours.

The purpose of moving all-in is that you want to see all five cards. I'm not a move-in player, but in certain situations (especially short-handed and late in the tournament) you have to do it. Suppose that a player raises, you call with the A-K, and the flop comes 7-4-2. Your opponent makes a bet — now you have to give up the hand. If you make a decision to play A-K short-handed, you move in with it because you want to see all five cards. (Of course, you might be up against someone who is holding aces, and then you know that you're in bad shape.)

THE RAISING HANDS FROM EARLY POSITION

For the percentage of times that you raise before the flop, there are very few times that you are reraised in no-limit hold'em. In the first four positions, the raising hands are big pairs — queens or better, *not* jacks or better — and A-K, if you feel good about the hand.

Nothing is wrong with making a small raise with A-K, but a lot of players who have moved up from limit hold'em to no-limit tournaments will move in with a big number of chips when they hold A-K. Why put all those chips in jeopardy when you don't have anything yet? Just make a standard raise.

For example, if you're still in the first round with $25 and $50 blinds, bring it in for $200 or $300. I've seen novice players bring in the A-K for $4,000 or $5,000 with everybody on the board sitting behind them. What if somebody behind them wakes up with aces or kings? Tom notes that, in a case where you have overbet the pot, you're not going to get action unless you're beaten. You're either going to win $75 (the blinds) or lose a ton of chips.

THE STARTING HANDS IN MIDDLE POSITION

You can lower your standards a little when you are in middle position — seats five, six, and seven in nine-handed play. You can play a hand such as A-10 *suited* or above if all of the players in front of you have passed — The A-10 is one hand that I recommend playing suited. If I were going to play a big ace (A-10 on up), the hand would need to be suited because of that slight edge that it gives you in possibly flopping a flush. You still have players behind you, so you have to be able to stand a raise.

You always should ask yourself, "If I play this hand and get raised, can I play it?" Obviously, it is *who* raises you that affects your decision.

You need to be watching how the flow of the game is going, what kinds of cards your opponents are playing. Are they the types who would be likely to raise you with a K-Q or K-J, or maybe a baby ace (an ace with a small kicker)? You have to be observant enough to know those answers. When you bring in a hand like A-10 or above from a middle position, and you're not bringing it in for a raise, obviously you're just hoping to catch a flop.

THE AMOUNT OF THE RAISE

There are three reasons to raise in no-limit hold'em: To get more money in the pot (get a call), to isolate, or to try to win the pot right there. If there are four limpers in the pot and you have a big pair, you want to reduce the number of players to one or two, so you make a big enough raise to guarantee it. You don't want the limpers to flop two rag pairs, for example, and beat your big pair, so you try to get them out before the flop.

No-limit is a game in which you never actually have to build a pot. When you move in on them, there are a lot of players who will call a raise for all of their chips with a hand like A-Q. They're not good players, but they are out there.

Tom says that if he is the first one in the pot and decides to bring it in for a raise, he makes the raise three to five times the size of the big blind. If someone already has trailed in, he scales the raise upward a notch or so.

HOW MUCH WILL THEY CALL?

When you want a call, another way to do it is to make a raise that is the size that you think your opponents will call. Some players will stand a bigger raise than others if they decide to play a hand, so you make the raise the size that you think they will play. Player A might be the type who will call you for $300; Player B might call if you raise as much as $600. These are the types of things that you learn from observation.

Players who are new to no-limit play often ask whether they should base the size of their raise on the amount of chips that they have in front of them. No, the only time that you use a percentage of your chips to determine how much you raise is when you're at the final table with, say, five players left.

Say that there are two tables left and there are five players at each table. You're playing down to the final nine players who will go to the last table. You pick up a hand such as two tens, two jacks, or two queens and you decide to raise the pot.

Now you have to make a decision: If you raise the pot, are you willing to play for all of your chips? In this case, I would raise with at least one-half of my chips, if I didn't put them all in to begin with, to try to shut them all out. Or, you might want somebody to play with a lesser pair. If somebody makes a play back at you, you are pot-committed. You have made sure that you're mentally committed to this pot. And then you simply go with it.

Frequently, I see players bring in two queens or two jacks for $400-or-so, somebody will re-pop it, and then they throw away their big pairs. It happens time and time again. About a quarter of the time, you will lay down the best hand, because you're playing smart poker. But when you are playing five-handed or less in a poker tournament and you're getting short on chips, you want to commit yourself to the pot when you bring it in for a raise.

When you raise with one-half or more of your chips, you know that you're going to go for the rest of them if you have to.

SETTING THE STANDARD

How much you raise in no-limit hold'em is fairly standard. One player at the table usually sets the standard at each particular level. Whoever makes the first big raise sets the standard. Say that we're anteing a quarter ($25) and the blinds are $100 and $200, making $525 in the pot to start with. If I were going to raise, I would make it $700; in other words, a little bit more than the total money in the pot. Usually, in cases like this, for whatever the amount of my first raise, the other players will follow that standard.

VARYING THE SIZE OF YOUR BETS

Since you're playing no-limit, you can vary the size of your bets according to the players you're up against, whereas in pot-limit, your raises must be a standard size. This is one reason why no-limit hold'em is a much better game for top players. Pot-limit has more skill to it than limit poker, but no-limit has far more skill than pot-limit. The real art in pot-limit is in building a pot, but in no-limit, you don't have to do that. Your goal is to extricate as much money from your opponent as you can, and there are a lot of ways of doing that.

At any time, all of your chips can be in jeopardy in no-limit—on the flop, on fourth street, and at fifth street. A lot of times in no-limit hold'em, when people flop big hands, there is no action until fifth street, but then there may be a lot of it.

There are players who will move their raises around, bet $600 one time, $1,500 the next, $1,000 on another hand. They are giving out information by varying the size of their raise. So, I suggest that you always raise by about the same amount, an amount that is commensurate with the level that you are at. In this way, people cannot use the amount of your raise to pigeonhole you on a hand. Some people have used three-to-four times the size of the big blind to gauge the size of their raises, but I don't use that method because I always know the size of the pot.

Say that you're anteing $100 and the blinds are $300-$600. At that level, it is costing you $1,800 in antes and blinds every nine hands to play the round. All of these types of things are factored into your tournament play because they begin to eat into your stack very heavily.

You can pick up more pots as the limits get higher. You have to pick them up just to stay alive. And so, I probably would bring it in for $2,000 at this level, just a little bit more than what is in the pot. That's enough to make people stop and think, "Do I want to risk $2,000 to play this hand? Am I willing to sacrifice $2,000 to possibly win $4,000?"

One top player that I know who does well in these situations will move in all of his chips when he's sitting in back. He doesn't do it from the front, just from around the back. He might have $25,000 sitting in front of him, have two sixes in his hand, and move all of them in from, say, sixth or seventh position because he is the first to act. He will even do it with A-6. He makes a monster opening raise to pick up the blinds. He thinks that he has the best hand, and he is afraid to get played with— he just wants to win the blinds. But to sacrifice $25,000 to win $4,000 doesn't make much sense to me.

The thought that I keep in my mind all of the time is that if the first four hands don't have anything, there is a chance that the last five players *do* have something. So, if you're in middle to late position and the action is passed to you, why would you put in all of your money? Unless, of course, you do it as a flat bluff.

BLUFFING

People's perception of bluffing in no-limit hold'em is that "The bluff is king," as Tex Sheahan used to say in his poker columns. But let me tell you that there is less bluffing being done than most people think. Before the flop, the bluff positions are the button and the little blind. More bluffing is done from those positions than from any other spot. Although I can't say that I never bluff from the button or the small blind, most of the time, I try to use a reverse from those positions — I want to be in a bluff position *with* a hand so that my opponents will think that I am bluffing and someone with a weaker hand will call me.

I bluff as much or more than most people, but I like to bluff from a different position than the so-called standard ones. For example, you can bluff from the first seat; I've done it lots of times. When you come in for a raise under the gun, that's a strength position. You don't want to put in all of your chips, just a good-sized raise.

Unless you can show them a hand, you can't bluff from any position . You have to be able to show them a hand when you are called. Tom mentions that a front position bluff or semi-bluff usually is tried when you just need to pick up a pot. It's a far stronger bluff because your opponents are going to give you credit for a hand because you raised from the front. Of course, it's far riskier than bluffing from the back.

If an unknown player, or one that you don't consider to be a top player (and who isn't a maniac), puts in a front position raise, you usually can give him more credit for having a hand that you can give to someone like me or Tom. If a player like that raises from the front, I can guarantee you that I will throw my hand away unless I have kings or aces. A player like Barbara Enright, who understands position, might put in a bluff or semi-bluff raise from the first seat in a shorthanded game, but she will never do it without a hand in a full ring. She can be an absolute machine gunner, but she also can settle down when she needs to. She can play very solid poker, and she understands the importance of position very well.

All of the big pots usually are hand against hand, big bluff against big bluff. To use an old Southern poker expression, it's the old "iron balls" theory: Most of the top players have guts. They are not afraid to put a man on a certain hand and then sacrifice all of their chips on a bluff. It's really a grandstand play and, with me, it happens at least once in a tournament.

Say that you have put in a raise and your opponent comes over the top of you for a decent reraise. You know that he doesn't have aces or kings; you have him on a hand, but not aces or kings. So, you have the guts to come back over the top of him and make him lay down his hand. This type of move happens, but you have to be willing to take that kind of a chance. When you're talking about bluffing, that is the ultimate bluff.

You're not likely to take that kind of a chance early in the tournament, but at some time during the event, a situation will come up when you can do it. And even though you absolutely know your man, and you absolutely know that the situation is right, you're still taking a chance because anybody can pick up two aces or two kings and bust you.

Again, it all depends on the "feel" factor, your timing. I don't care if you wrote fifty books about poker, you still couldn't teach a person that little thing that you are born with. "Feel" gives the top players an edge over the next-to-the-top players. It separates the men from the boys, not in the sense of gender, but in the sense of being superior versus being very good at poker.

I hate to tell you how many tournaments I've survived in without holding any cards, by just strategically picking up a pot here and there to stay alive. Sometimes, you can come out of the first seat raising. It's a bad play, of course, but when you raise from the first seat, your opponents give you credit for a powerful hand. (You've got to have iron balls to do it, of course.)

But just remember one thing: If you cannot show winning hands, you cannot bluff in poker. If players see that you're not catching anything, you sure as hell cannot bluff them. The only way that you can bluff in pot-limit and no-limit poker is if you're able to show a bunch of hands, because then the other players will give you credit for a hand. But if they see that you can't win a pot, and you're swinging at the pot, you don't have much of a chance.

THE LUCK FACTOR

Kenny Flaton was the last one with a chance to win the car at the Bicycle Club's tournament in 1996. If he won the tournament, he would win the all-around best player award and the car, so he wasn't giving one dime away. Kenny brought in the pot for a decent raise and Paul Ladanyi reraised him. Flaton went over the top for all of his chips. Paul had the 7-4 of hearts in his hand. Flaton had the "two eyes of Texas," just what he was supposed to have (aces). For no reason that I could see, Paul put in all of his chips, ended up making three sevens, and busted Kenny out of the tournament at a time when Paul himself could have been knocked out with the play.

Later in the tournament, Paul moved all-in over a raise by another player with a Q-9. Against the other man's A-K, the Q-9 won the pot. Another situation came up between Paul and me when I had two nines. I raised up the pot three-handed with the nines and he moved all in over the top of me holding a Q-10. I called him. At least he had two overcards in this situation, but there is no way that he could have known this. The flop came K-Q-10, giving him queens and tens. But on fourth street came a jack, giving me a straight. Then on fifth street came another 10, giving him a full house. I hadn't hesitated to call him because I had observed all of the other hands that he had played.

I had all of this in the back of my mind during the first no-limit tournament at the Commerce Club's L. A. Poker Championship in 1997. Paul raised on the button three or four times, and I came back over the top of him three or four times to take the pot away from him. Most of those times, I had a hand but on a few of them, I didn't. I said to myself, "Now I'm setting this man up; he's going to make a play at me." In no-limit, you can set up plays and opponents by your previous plays. That's why I'll show a hand once in a while when I have bluffed. I want someone to see my hand. It's like the finely coiled cobra just waiting for somebody to open the lid on the basket.

Then, a hand came down in which Paul brought it in and I made a small raise. He said, "All in!" I had $42,000 at the time and he had $24,000. All I had was A-J offsuit, but in my mind, there was no doubt that I had the best hand, so I called him. You have to show your hand when you're all-in at the final table in a tournament. He turned over a 9-6 offsuit.

My play was exactly right. My timing was right. I had set him up. I was a 2-to-1 favorite, and that's big enough to get in all of your money before the flop. The flop came 9-9-8. Paul wound up winning the hand and the tournament.

This is just another example that shows how the luck factor comes into play. You can set up all the plays in the world, you can play perfectly on a hand, and you can still lose. And there's nothing that you can do about it.

THE CLOCK

Some players wear a watch with a miniature alarm function that gives them a 10-minute warning toward the end of each round so that they know how much time is left in the round. Sometimes at the start of a new round, players who have been playing in an ultra-conservative fashion, start going to the center with what appears to be reckless abandon, especially in no-limit tournaments. For people who have been watching all of the prior conservative action from the rail, it seems like a bell has gone off and people are now racing to the center with all of their chips.

A good example of this occurs on the first level of

day two in the championship event at the WSOP. The blinds are $100-$200 with $25 antes at the end of the first day, but on the second day, everything doubles. When the blinds go to $200-$400 with a $50 ante, players who were just sitting patiently during day one realize that they can't sit around any more because they're getting blinded to death. There are more casualties on the first round of day two (the fifth round of the tournament) than there are on any other round.

The tournament is played down to twenty-seven people on the second day. The result of having the blinds and antes double at the beginning of each round on the second day is that these middle rounds in the WSOP tournament are speeded up, not because they have shorter time limits but because the blinds and antes are increasing at a faster rate. Because entries have increased dramatically during the past few years at the WSOP, these blind and ante increases on day two have helped it to conclude within its four-day time limit.

Conservative play usually is correct and is the norm for day one because the blinds are still relatively small, but with this emphasis on faster play during day two, a similar approach will not get the money. You can hang on for a long time on day one with conservative play, but the time factor clicks in on day two. By the end of day one, approximately 45 percent of the field has been eliminated. After the first round of day two, the field usually gets pared down to fewer than one-third of the original entrants. The carnage during those first two hours of day two is quite extensive.

When the increases in blinds and antes are more gradual, the clock is less of a factor in your game strategy. But when the increases begin to double at the beginning of each new round, the clock becomes far more important and you can't just sit there and hope that a conservative approach will come through for you. This is true of all the major tournaments. Any time the tournament gets to about the fourth or fifth level of play when the blinds and antes double at every round, you can't just sit there any longer playing conservatively and hope to be successful; you have to reevaluate your strategy.

Of course, the larger your stack, the less concern you have for the clock at any level. I am more concerned about the clock when I have a short stack because the blinds and antes can eat you alive, so you have to think about the clock when you're short-stacked. If you're quite a way into the tournament (when the blinds and antes are doubling up every round), you know that you're going to be playing shorthanded pretty soon because a lot of players will be dropping out.

I have also won a lot of the last hands at the end of a level. I know that people are itching to get up and take a break, so the last few hands in the round are sometimes good places to pick up a pot here and there. Before the final add-on when you can still rebuy in a rebuy tournament, there is often a three-minute warning, then a two-minute warning, and then a bell rings for the final hand to be dealt. Many times, players will make risky plays at this point, trying to either accumulate chips or avoid a rebuy. So, during these last few hands, you sometimes will see some surprising hands being played, with players taking the risk of going broke.

THE IMPORTANCE OF STACK SIZE

Everybody starts off equal. The more chips you have in relation to the size of the blinds, the less reason you have to play in big pots without premium hands because there isn't enough money in the middle to steal or to fight over.

Depending on what stage of the tournament you are playing, your stack size matters. It doesn't affect your play in the first few levels because your basic strategy isn't much different from ring games, even in a tournament with a very big buy-in such as a WSOP event. From the second level on, as chips begin to get redistributed, tournament strategy becomes more important. Then the style of play begins changing rapidly from the third or fourth level onward. The further you go, the more that tournament considerations and chip counts come into play. And when the antes start going into effect, the chips really begin to get redistributed.

During the early stage, I don't worry about knocking anybody out. In fact, I don't care if I ever knock anybody out, just as long as I knock out the second-to-last player. You should be more concerned with adding to your chip count in the early rounds than eliminating players. Don't worry about what you have in chips, just let it happen. Don't force the action. Don't be thinking, "Well, that one guy has $8,000 and I only have $1,000 and I have to get up to his level, and so I'm going to force the action." If you do that, you might start playing hands you shouldn't play. Things will come to you sooner or later.

PLAYING A MEDIUM STACK

Tom discusses the importance of stack size in *Championship Tournament Poker*. He states that you have the most decisions to make when you have a medium stack. When you are short-stacked, you are limited in your options because you know that you're probably going to get played with. With a big stack, you have a lot more options and fewer critical decisions to make. You're not going to play a big pot against any other huge stack unless you have a premium hand, but you're going to take more latitude against the shorter stacks.

But when you have a medium stack, you're stuck in between these two strategies. Your decisions are of major importance, just as they are when you're short-stacked. Playing a medium stack is something like playing marginal hands—it can make the difference in a win or a loss.

What separates the men from the boys is how they play the medium stacks to try to inch up to a big stack status and avoid becoming short-stacked. Some of the very great players are terrific big-stack players, but they aren't so good at playing a short stack.

Players like Men Nguyen, John Bonetti, and Phil Hellmuth play a big stack devastatingly effectively, but they are not as efficient in short-stack play. These are all aggressive players who like to bludgeon you with a tall stack, and when they get short-stacked, their weapons are taken away from them. On the other hand, Mansour Matloubi is a genius with a short stack, but is not as strong with a big stack.

STACK SIZE AND TOURNAMENT STAGE

How you play a stack also depends on what stage of the tournament you are playing. I think that you ought to set up criteria for what kinds of hands you will play at any time in the tournament with any size of stack in the early rounds, during the middle, and at the end. You need to have criteria for the hands that you're willing to play, and I believe that your criteria override the size of stack that you have.

Early in the tournament, my stack size usually doesn't influence the hands that I play, whereas late in the tournament, it does. If you're in a short-stack situation where the blinds can eat you alive, for instance, you're going to have to find something that you're willing to play before you get so short-stacked that if you double up, it doesn't help you. You want to get your money in before you're anteed down to the point where you have enough for the ante but even if you double up, you will have only enough left for the next two hands.

PLAYING A SHORT STACK

With a short stack, the idea is to stay alive. So, you have to pick out your situations. There are certain players that you want to play pots against and you can tell who's running over the game. These are the types of players that you shoot at because you can play a less than premium hand against them. You also can easily tell which players are playing premium hands. Hopefully, you still will be in a big ring when you're short-stacked because then you will have more time to pick out your players. But if you're on a shorthanded table, you just have to find two cards that you like and go with them.

Of course, I've been talking about playing short-stacked late in the tournament. Early in the tournament, the blinds aren't going to hurt you, so why should you worry if you have a short stack? Suppose you look over the table and you see one guy who has $2,000 and another one with $3,000. You've got $400. That's a short stack, but so what? You're only two hands away from being tied with the bigger stacks.

Now, suppose you're at the final table with a short stack. You still must find a hand and go with it ... but I usually try to ramrod them. I'll put my game in "stop save." I'm not doing the calling, I'm doing the betting. Tom explains that this means that you try to be the initiator — you don't react to them, you make *them* react to you. You put the pressure on your opponents and force them to make the decision.

PLAYING A BIG STACK

With a big stack at the last table, you play more conservatively than you do with a short stack. You look around the table and see who can do what. Then you say to yourself, "The top three's where the money is. I'll open up when I get to the top three."

With a medium stack at the final table, you still don't have to hurry. All you want to catch is fifty percent of the hands, not 60 percent. If you break even, you still can win. If I have a medium stack against a couple of large stacks, I'm not worried about those big stacks because if I hold any hands at all, I'm going to have a large stack, too. I can double up through those big stacks.

Obviously, with a short stack at the final table, I'm not worried about the players—I'm only worried about my stack size, because the blinds and antes can eat me live. And that's why I'm ramming and jamming.

MOVING UP THE LADDER

Every rung that you can move up the ladder at the final table in the WSOP means a big jump in money. There is a big increase in money from ninth to eighth to seventh to sixth, and right on up the ladder, because there is so much money in the tournament. But in any other tournament, the bottom six don't win diddledy-squat, so you're less concerned about moving up from, say, seventh to sixth place. You're only concerned about moving up from fourth to third, or third to second, in the smaller tournaments.

Even at the WSOP where there are significant increases in money for each place you move up, these increases are nothing like the massive increase in money paid for the last three spots.

This is why I'm never concerned about how many players I can knock out of a tournament. The only person that I care about knocking out is the one that I get head-up with at the final table. If I can knock him out, I'll win it all. If it happens, it happens. In 1992, the year that Tom finished second to Men Nguyen in seven-card stud at the WSOP, he never eliminated a single player from start to finish.

PLAYING A PATIENT GAME

People have a tendency to get nervous during a tournament. When they do, they start making mistakes, and no-limit hold'em is a game of mistakes. If other players aren't making mistakes, you aren't going to win. If *you* aren't making mistakes, *they* aren't going to win.

All top players not only make fewer mistakes, they also capitalize on other people's mistakes. If you don't play perfect poker (or don't get extremely lucky) against top players, they will beat you. None of the top players think of themselves as being lucky—if anything, they think of themselves as being unlucky.

Tom has observed that no-limit hold'em probably is the most patient of all the poker games. Being patient is good up to a point. But if you're too patient—if you wait so long for a playable hand that your chips start growing cobwebs—you aren't going to get there very often because you're playing too tight and, therefore, your play is too predictable. You have to be very flexible as situations arise while you are going through the stages of a tournament. This is why some otherwise good poker players who do well in cash games do not do exceptionally well in tournaments.

You cannot play the same style all the time in a tournament, you must adapt to the ebb and flow of the competition.

MATH AND POKER

The math of poker should be in the back of your mind all the time. For most of the top pros, it is automatic. They can make their decisions quickly because they understand the numbers. But when you watch some players, you can practically see the numbers clicking in their eyes. You can tell that they are methodically figuring out things in their minds:

"Is the pot laying me enough odds to make such

and such a play? What are my chances? What's the math behind my hand?" That type of intense deliberation can be a big tell on somebody, a huge tell, because you know that they have a hand that they're trying to compute. The hand isn't strong enough for them to know immediately whether to play it. It's a "decision" hand that they're trying to figure out whether to play based on pot odds and other things.

In tournament poker, pot odds isn't always the most important factor in deciding whether to play a hand. It goes out the window a lot of times because you can't go back to your pocket for more chips—and that should be a determining factor in each and every hand. You should take the math into consideration, yes, but if that's all you're thinking about—and you forget about the fact that if you don't win the pot, you will either be out of the tournament or you will take a big hit to your stack—you are putting too much importance on it. Your thinking in critical tournament situations has to be different from how you think in a side game.

You should know what you're going to do with whatever card comes out before that card is dealt so that, most of the time, you will be able to act fast on your hand and not give away anything. Very few times do I take any time at all on a hand because I'm aware of what cards will help me and which ones won't help me. And I know what I'm going to do if those cards come out. In other words, when I go into a hand, I have already planned what my play is going to be after the flop, depending on the number of players in the hand.

THE NATURE OF NO-LIMIT POTS

Most of the pots that you will play in no-limit hold'em tournaments are going to be two-way hands, except in the early stages when there might be some four and five-way hands. A lot of players limp early in the tournament. Although some of them are limping in with drawing hands, my whole idea is to let *them* play the drawing hands, not me. I'm trying *not* to play them.

I got knocked out of the WSOP one time on a drawing hand. I was in the big blind with A♠ 5♠. Gabe Kaplan had brought it in from the first seat for $200 during the second level of play. There were five callers when it got around to me and so I threw in $150 to make the call. The flop came A-3-4, with the 3♠ 4♠. I had top pair, a straight draw, and a straight flush draw. I checked from the blind, Gabe made a big bet at the pot, and I moved all in on him with a check raise.

He had the other two aces in the hole, and I missed all my draws. In this situation, if I hadn't put in the $150 to start with—get me right, when I *knew* I didn't have the best hand—I would have still been in the tournament instead of getting broke on the hand. In that instance, I was thinking, "Well, I've got pot odds," and that's what made me play it.

Tom observed that many times in this situation, I would have won that pot with the check raise, and that when I got called, I knew I had the worst hand at the moment, but with so many outs, I still had a chance of winning it. I played my hand on the flop the way that it should have been played, but the big question came up *before* the flop.

When you have a questionable calling hand, you have to ask yourself, "What am I hoping to flop?" There have been many times in ring games when I have called with a hand like the 6♥5♥ in a raised pot from around back with four or five players already in the pot. I'd hate to tell you how many times I've flopped a straight and a flush draw with a hand like that, and never made a dime with it.

When you get the big flop, what are you trying to make? Say the flop comes 3-4-8 with two hearts when you're holding the 6♥ 5♥. Now you're going to play the hand, and probably play it strongly. But if you hadn't played the 6-5 to begin with, you wouldn't have been in any trouble. What you really have is just a six-high hand.

PLAYING THE ACE-KING AFTER THE FLOP

The Ace-King is the most misplayed hand in no-limit poker. Say that you have raised with Ace-King from a front spot and one or two people have called. The board comes with 9-7-3, three suits. What do you do with your A-K? I don't care whether or not I've raised before the flop, I never bet A-K when the flop comes three rags.

If you've raised the pot going in, your opponent(s) has some kind of hand or he wouldn't have called you. He didn't have a raising hand or he would have reraised before the flop, so you can put him on anything from queens on down in the pairs (or maybe an A-Q or A-J), but it is more likely that he holds a pair. Now, if you fire at this hand, he's liable to raise you or call you ... and you don't have anything.

By betting, you have shut off your opportunity to get

a free turn card and possibly make your hand. If you check-check, you have found out information without it costing you anything. An aggressive player like Phil Hellmuth may have a tendency to fire on the flop head-up; that's his style of play. But you can burn up a lot of chips that way. I don't continue with A-K unless I flop a hand that relates to it in some way, a hand with some strength to it.

AGAINST AN ACE-RAG-RAG FLOP

Now suppose that the flop comes A-6-3. Perfect! The only hands that you are afraid of on this flop are two aces in the hole, or two treys or two sixes in the hole, so you are definitely going to bet the hand. It is more likely that you'll run into exactly the type of hand that you want to go up against, an A-Q or A-J. You are not trying to shut your opponents out of the pot. You don't mind a call — You *want* a call. So, you want to bet enough so that you can either win the pot or get called because, obviously, you are trying to maximize the amount that you can win on the hand.

If the board pairs the treys on the turn, that would be perfect. If your opponent has a trey or a set, you're already beaten anyway, and there's nothing that you can do about that. But if he has A-Q or A-J, he probably will say to himself, "I have a big kicker, so I'll call." And that's exactly what you want to happen.

WHEN A PAINT COMES ON THE TURN

As long as a picture card doesn't come on the board, you're in good shape. But if a picture card does come out after your opponent has called you on the flop (a jack or a queen, for example), you had better shut down, because then you have a decision to make about the other player.

If he bets, the best hand that you usually can have is a tie, with both of you holding an A-K. But there are a lot of other hands that he can have. You might be surprised at how many players will call you and not give you the ace when it flops. They may think that you're betting an underpair and they have two queens or jacks in the hole. Then a queen comes off on the turn and, boy o' boy, you're in trouble. So, you must be very careful if a paint comes on fourth street.

When a paint doesn't come off, you want to make a fourth-street bet that is big enough to lose your opponent because you don't mind losing him at this point. You've already made money on the hand, and you don't want to give him a shot at making a double pair. So, you make a pretty good-sized bet on fourth street — if he calls, make him pay to do it.

A major axiom in no-limit hold'em is "Always make them pay to chase you." Bobby Hoff once said about me, "T. J. *will* make them look at their hole cards." I suggest that you do the same thing.

AGAINST A DRAWING HAND

Even if an opponent has a drawing hand, you have distorted the pot so much that no drawing hand could be profitable. About the only type of drawing hand that could be out there on this flop example (A-6-3) is a 4-5. It is very unlikely that someone would be playing in a raised pot with a 4-5, but it does happen. You also come across certain players who will play "Any Ace" — A-6, A-4, A-8, and so on. But you *know* that about them, and take it into consideration.

In this example, if the river card is anything below a ten without pairing the board again, you come at it with another bet. But once again, you should be very fearful if it comes with a queen or jack, or even a ten in some situations. Of course, you should know which players will play tens or A-10.

WHEN THE FLOP COMES WITH RAGS

Now, let's change the scenario: The action is two-handed, but you're sitting *behind* the other player. Remember that in no-limit hold'em, position is always power. The flop comes three rags and your opponent checks to you. You don't bet: You check right back at him. That way, you're not shutting yourself out. For example, what will you do if he checks, you bet, and then he raises you? What are you going to do with your hand *then*? So, you may as well take the opportunity that his check has given you and get a free card by checking along.

On fourth street, you might hit an ace or king. If he checks again, you can fire at him. But once you don't hit your hand, all of a sudden the brakes go on and you're trying to play a small pot. Hopefully, the other guy has an ace and you can play a showdown. If he bets, all that you can lose is your original raise. Or when he bets, you might decide that you have the best hand and call him. It all depends on the circumstances. But at least you have left all of your options open by checking along on the flop.

Someone suggested that this is an example of playing the waiting game, but that's not it. This is an example of playing the hand the way that it should be played. Why take a chance and put all of your chips in jeopardy, especially in a tournament, when you don't have anything?

A lot of players will fire at the pot one time in these types of situations. When they see a baby flop, here they come! But I think they're making a mistake when they do that: You have to give an opponent credit for having something to have been able to call your raise to start with. If the board comes nine- high, he might have that board beaten; he might be in there with tens or jacks or queens, which aren't reraising hands anyway. You could be setting yourself up to lose a lot of money on the hand.

If a guy bets in front of me against that nine-high flop when I'm holding the A-K, he wins the pot. It's that simple. I don't *care* what he has, he wins it right there. As far as I'm concerned, A-K is A-K and two deuces beat A-K. It's a powerful hand if you can flop to it, but it isn't much of a hand when you don't.

BIG PAIRS AFTER THE FLOP

Aces, kings, and queens are *big* pairs. If you have raised before the flop with two aces, kings, or queens, and no overcards come on the flop, it is correct to make a bet in no-limit hold'em. But you have to keep in mind that all you have is an overpair. You have to know the players that you are playing with, so that if somebody comes back over the top of you, you can decide what to do with your hand. Are you going to call or throw it away?

If you lead bet and get raised on the flop, you must decide whether you're going to go through with your pair or throw it away. Assuming that there are no draws on the board, there is a pretty good chance that your opponent has either a set or two pair, or he may have called your raise with some crazy hand. Suppose you have pocket kings and the flop comes Q-J-6. Your first worry is that your opponent has flopped a set, although he could also have two pair, queens and jacks. Or if he's a weak player, he could have any two pair.

Remember that some weak players call raises with any two connectors or suited cards. If someone has raised in front of you before the flop and that player leads at the pot on the flop, you definitely don't try to shut him out then. You smooth call him. If you are the one who leads on the flop and an opponent who is a *player* smooth calls your bet, an alarm should go off in your head— "Boy, I'd better shut down now." You have to ask yourself why he has called you.

More mistakes are made in these types of situations than almost anywhere else. A player will go through with the hand and then a deuce comes on fourth street, for example. Thinking that his opponent might have a drawing hand such as a K-10, the lead bettor makes a big bet at the pot to try to shut him out. If you make that kind of bet and your opponent comes over the top of you, you're a gone goose.

Always remember that all of your chips are in jeopardy on any one hand, so play smart. Know when to give credit, when to shut down. These judgments all come from knowing your opponents. Everything in this book evolves from the first chapter on knowing how your opponents play in different situations. If you've been in a tournament for three or four hours, you've already seen a lot of situations come up that give you information about how your opponents play.

WHEN YOU FLOP A SET

Now suppose that you flop your set. Whether it is top set or middle set makes a big difference. Say that you called a pre-flop raise with two jacks from a back position, and the flop comes A-J-6. Your opponent leads at the pot. You're pretty sure that he has a big ace or an overpair to your jacks such as kings or queens, so you don't try to shut him out.

In this case, I would flat call his bet; I'm not going to move in on him at this point. Columbus took a chance, so I'm going to take one, too. If you're the first to act, you check to him. You see, in no-limit you're not trying to build a pot like you do in pot-limit, because the pot will take care of itself in no-limit.

Say that the board pairs on fourth street, which strengthens your opponent's hand if it pairs one of the bottom cards on the board. If one of the top cards pairs, he's going to shut down anyway. If you had tried to shut him down on the flop, you would only have won what was already in the pot. But if any normal card comes off on the turn, he may bet again because you only flat called the flop. Then there are some chips in the pot and you have a chance of winning some real money, so you can raise him to maximize what you can win on the hand.

The only thing that's going to beat you on this flop is a set of aces. If your opponent has flopped the aces, you're gone, of course—but you're going to play the hand anyway. In no-limit hold'em, it's very hard to get away from a set. But suppose that your opponent bets, you raise, and he reraises you. You have to make a decision right there as to whether you have the best hand or only second-best set. In a side game, it's hard to lay down your set, but in a tournament, it's easier to do. I have laid down sets, and I'm sure that other players have, too.

THE CHECK CALL AND THE FLAT CALL

There is quite a difference between the check call from a front position, and the flat call from a late position. When you're in a back position and just flat call a bet with a strong hand, it makes your hand look weaker than when you check call.

A lot of times, a check call will ring a bell in your opponent's head and lead him to believe that you're slow playing, whereas a flat call from a late position is just everyday action and shouldn't ring any alarms in his head. The check call is a little stronger than a flat call.

So, in the situation discussed above, when you flop the set of jacks and are sitting in back of your opponent, you just flat call and hope that he bets again.

If he doesn't come again, you have two options: You can bet on fourth street, hoping that he will call; or you can wait until fifth street, which might weaken your hand in his eyes, and hope that your delayed bet will induce him to call. If he does lead on fourth street, you might just call him again, unless he bets big, in which case you might shut him out right there. If he bets first on the river, then you come over the top of him. The whole idea is to extricate the most money out of his stack.

THE RAISING HANDS AND THE RERAISING HANDS

Referring back to our earlier discussions, you know by now which players will bring it in for raises with smaller pairs. Unless you have an opponent pigeonholed as a player who often raises with small pairs, the only two hands that you can reraise the pot with are kings and aces. Queens definitely are out of the question, unless you're against the small-pair raiser, or unless you're sitting in a favorable position.

Suppose the player in the number-one seat brings it in for a raise and you're sitting in third position with two queens. If you reraise from this spot, you still have six players sitting behind you who could have aces or kings and might re-pop you, in which case you could really get in a lot of trouble with your queens.

There is nothing wrong with flat calling with two queens or two jacks. You save your reraises for when the table is down to three or four-handed. With the medium-large pairs—tens, jacks, or queens—you might want to reraise with these hands shorthanded, something that you never would do in a full ring.

Although aces and kings are the only two hands that you can reraise with, there are two ways of playing them. I often play "second-hand low" with aces and kings, and take a chance on them. In second-hand low, somebody brings it in for a raise when you have kings or aces in a position that is very close to the original bettor, who is sitting up front. You flat call and hope that somebody behind you will raise the pot and drive him back in to you so that you can really put it to him before the flop. Or I might make a minimal raise that I know won't hurt my stack. Then, if I don't flop to them, I can get rid of them anyway.

PLAYING POCKET ACES

Cardinal rule number one in no-limit hold'em is: *If you limp with aces, you will never get broke with aces.* The only reason that you limp with aces before the flop is so that someone behind you will raise and give you the opportunity to reraise. If you flat call with them before the flop and nobody raises, four or five players may limp into the pot behind you with all sorts of random hands. The more people in the pot, the more chance that you're going to get beaten. So, if one of them comes out swinging on the flop, you can simply throw your aces away and you haven't lost anything except your original bet. Nobody has seen your hand; nobody knows that you have limped in with aces, so just throw them away.

If you're in the stage of a tournament when you have a shorter stack than your opponents, you would be a fool to limp with aces. In this scenario, you have to raise with them because you don't have a lot of chips, and it means something to you when you play a pot.

But if you have a lot of chips and decide to limp with aces, you haven't really lost anything except your original bet if you lose with them. You want to *protect* your big stack, and try to *build* your short stack. With a big stack, you also could raise a pretty big amount to start with if you wanted to gamble with your aces.

Just remember the rule: If you limp with aces, you never get broke with aces, but I see it happen time and time again. Two aces are the best starting hand you can get, but when two small pair are out there, all you have is one pair of aces, Eke and Ike, American Airlines.

RERAISING WITH ACE-KING

On the button, you sometimes can reraise with A-K suited or even offsuit, but this type of raise is just a power play. In a power play, you raise enough money so that, hopefully, you can win the pot *before* the flop. You don't want to see the flop, but if you have, you have to. And if you are forced to see it, chances are that you will have at least one (or maybe two) overcards on your opponents, so you're not dead. Anytime that you make this play, you're only hoping to win what is already in the pot.

Time and time again, I see players raise the pot with A-K in a full ring. Then somebody moves in on them and beats them for the pot. I sometimes see the A-K call a reraise and get away with it, but I think that this is a horrible play, because most of the time, the A-K is taking much the worst of it. With a decent amount of chips, this is an especially bad move because when someone moves in on you after you have raised with A-K, then you are *calling* all of your money with A-K. There is quite a difference in raising and calling with this hand.

The situation is different when you're playing shorthanded: Then, A-K becomes a very powerful hand; A-Q becomes a powerful hand. The fewer the players, the less strength you usually will need to play. You also have other things working for you in shorthanded play: Your chip position versus their chip position, and what money position both your opponents and you are in.

PLAYING THE SMALL PAIRS

In Dallas, when a player used to show down his hand and say, "I've got one small pair," it usually was two queens! Tom and I have different opinions on how to play the small pairs. We're going to discuss both of our points of view in this section.

Tom likes to limp in with the small pairs, tens on down to deuces, even from a front position. He sees them as strictly limping hands, unless he decides to take a shot at the blinds with them from a middle position on back, in which case he might bring them in for a small raise. He likes to mix up his play with them like this in a full ring.

Occasionally, he also will bring in the pot for a small raise with a pair such as sixes from a front position if he is the first one in the pot. If someone pops him with a modest raise and it looks like he'll be playing head-up, he mucks them. But if the reraiser makes a small raise with a lot of chips in front of him, Tom will call with a small pair in hope of flopping a set, knowing that most of the time, he will have to give them up.

If one or two players in the ring have been doing a lot of pre-flop raising, Tom will just pass with the small pairs. Usually, it is in the early stages of the tournament when there is still a lot of limping going on that he will slip in with them because he thinks that small pairs play the easiest of any other starting hand. If he doesn't flop a set, he can easily get away from them, although he may give some action if he flops an open-ended straight draw.

In no-limit, there are huge implied odds, especially in the early rounds when everybody has a lot of chips in relation to the size of the blinds. Tom isn't looking for a big pot in the first round of the tournament unless he has the nuts or close to it and he is looking to trap somebody who is holding a big hand such as aces or another big pair or a set.

In contrast, I am not going to play little pairs, eights and below, in the first three or four seats in a full ring. If I play them at all, I will only play them from the next five seats, and I am not going to raise with them in a full ring. First of all, I don't want to give away any information about my hand. When you're playing a small pair and there are two callers behind you, there is the chance that they might each have a pair or two big connectors, normal playing hands.

The reason for not raising with your small pair is that you hope to flop a set. You're not risking much money by just calling; and if you get raised, you can get rid of your hand. The perfect scenario would occur when you hold a pair of eights and the flop comes K-8-2. If your opponents are playing their hands strong, you can set them up pretty well against this type of flop.

I don't play small pairs in early position because I think that I will just be giving away my money. A lot of pots are raised in no-limit hold'em; very few are limp-limp-limp. You cannot stand a raise with the small pairs, especially early in the tournament. In the first part of the tournament, you have x-amount of dollars, and every dollar that you lose in a pot is a drain on chips that you could have used later to double or triple up when you have a big hand. I think along these lines all of the time. If anything, I might play the small pairs later in the tournament rather than early.

Suppose the blinds are $50 and I bring it in for $50.

Then somebody raises me $150 and I decide to take a shot at it. On the flop, I don't like my hand and have to give it up. Now I've wasted $200. Later on when I have a big hand with, maybe, two-way action, I could have turned that $200 into $600. That's how you accumulate chips in a tournament.

There is nothing wrong with playing the small pairs the way that Tom plays them, I want to emphasize that. It's just that I am thinking along different lines when I am playing them. As he has said, he is willing to take a risk with small pairs and even call a small raise with them. In situations where I am looking to save some bets, Tom is more willing to gamble a little bit. There certainly are more than two ways to play in almost every situation.

SMALL PAIRS AFTER THE FLOP

How you play small pairs after the flop depends upon the texture of the flop. Tom gives this example: "Say that you took the flop with a pair of pocket fours; you called a small raise or maybe two or three players limped in, probably with face cards. The flop comes 9-7-4. This is not a pot that I want to lead at because I want my opponents to catch something. If they all check, that's fine. I'm hoping that a face card will hit on the turn so that I can get some action. If the flop comes K-Q-4, it figures to hit somebody. In this scenario, I sometimes will lead at the pot in the hope that somebody will come after me. It all depends on what I think my opponents will do."

The K-Q-4 is a dangerous flop for you if you have flopped a set of fours. If somebody with pocket kings or queens has raised the pot before the flop, you have to be so careful with the hand, it's pitiful. You think that you have the best hand, but that isn't necessarily true. In this case, you have to play completely differently. You have to let their betting patterns and how they play the hand dictate the way that you play the hand. In an unraised pot, you can be less fearful that someone has limped in with pocket kings or queens, but in a raised pot there is always the danger that your opponent has raised with the big pocket pairs.

In an unraised pot, you can be 99 percent sure that you have the best hand, although someone occasionally will limp with kings or queens in the hole. This type of trap flop is just one more reason why I don't like to play baby pairs in early position. I realize that set over set doesn't come up very often, but it does happen. And when it happens, it will destroy you if you hold the low set.

I remember a hand that I played three-handed in a side game in Dallas against Bobby Hoff and Herschel from Houston. Herschel had raised ten pots in a row with anything from pocket deuces on up, but he limped into this pot. Bobby was on the button and he made a little raise (any time he's on the button, he makes a little courtesy raise). I was in the blind with two fours in the hole and decided to call. Herschel also called. The flop came 10-6-4. I checked, Herschel checked, and Bobby bet on the button. I knew that he had an overpair, because he would have checked if he hadn't hit it. Then I raised. Herschel reraised.

When Herschel reraised, he could have had anything, an overpair or something like that. Bobby studied for a long time, and then he folded his two queens. I was completely pot committed. Out of $5,000, I had $1,000 left in front of me. I called Herschel's reraise. He had limped in with two tens. This is the perfect example of a situation in which you can get trapped. My play was fine, but I was a gone goose.

JEOPARDY

You always are taking a chance of getting in jeopardy with the small pairs. Say that you are in the pot with pocket fours. The flop comes 2-3-5. Then how are you going to play the hand? You have second pair and an open-ended straight draw. Someone might play this hand, and sometimes play it very strongly, and never get there.

Tom says that in this scenario, he will check so that he can't get raised off the hand. Then if somebody bets at it, he might come back with a raise. But say that you lead with a pot-sized bet and somebody moves in on you. In a tournament, you cannot call, whereas in a side game, you might make the call or even lead at the pot. That's the difference between the two.

In my opinion, there are so many traps that you can fall into with small pairs that I play them very carefully. Tom thinks that there are more traps with the suited connectors than there are with small pairs, but of course, there are a lot of connectors that you never play.

SUITED CONNECTORS

Suited cards are what I refer to as "A Broke's Lament." As he leaves the table, a guy tells his buddy, "I got busted in this pot, but I was suited."

Players like that put tremendous value in holding two suited cards, the K♣ 5♣ or the A♥ 6♥. Believe me, the value in these hands is very slim unless you flop a flush to them, but some players will even call raises with them! With these types of hands, what do you want to hit except for a flush?

As far as I'm concerned, the only value in suited cards occurs when you are holding A-K, A-Q, or A-J. Being suited gives them a little extra added value. Their real value is in the ranks ... I am just as happy with unsuited A-K or A-Q or A-J as I am when they are suited. If you would not play any two cards unsuited, you have no reason to play them suited.

Suppose you're holding the K-Q suited and make a flush on the flop. Since your opponents probably have no redraws on an unpaired board, you win only what is in the pot if you bet it from up front. In actual play, the hand is over right then. Therefore, you have to check your flush from a front spot to slow down the action a little bit. Certainly, if your opponent makes a bet, you might raise him, although I may be more inclined to just flat call him, because I don't want to have to decide whether or not to play the hand for all my money. Also, you might be up against a bigger flush if your opponent has the ace-suited in his hand.

So, you always want to try to play these types of hands from a back position so that you will have more betting options. Personally, the big suited cards, A-K through A-J, are the only types of suited hands that I want to play. With the lower suited cards, you might make a flush, but your opponent may make a bigger flush. Certainly, you wouldn't play A-little suited; I don't even play it in limit hold'em.

A RULE FOR SUITED CARDS

The general rule is: If you wouldn't play any two cards unsuited, you should not play them suited. Of course, there are a few exceptions. For example, if several players have trailed into an unraised pot and you are on the button with King-small suited, you might call the pot in the hope of flopping the big flush. You never would call a raise, however.

The danger with playing this type of hand is that you might flop top pair, have the action get checked to you, and then you might be forced to make a little bet at the pot. Then you are leaving yourself wide open to a check raise and may wind up losing money with a hand that you shouldn't have played in the first place. Because of the likelihood of having this happen, I don't want to play hands like that; I don't want to put myself in that spot.

PLAYING THE SMALL CONNECTORS

When is it correct to call a raise with small connectors? When you are on the button or in the spot right in front of the button, with a lot of chips against a lot of chips, there is nothing wrong with calling a small raise with 4-5 suited, 6-7 suited, or 7-8 suited. Your opponents will never put you on this hand to start with, and if you don't flop to it, you can get rid of it right away. You're simply taking a shot at busting somebody with your small suited connectors. You not only can do this in multiway pots, you sometimes can do it head-up in a big stack-against-big stack situation.

But this is the only time that I am going to play small

connectors; I am never going to open a pot with them.

What if you flop a draw to this type of hand? As I've said before, I try to stay away from as many draws in no-limit hold'em as I possibly can, especially in tournaments. In tournaments, *draws are death.* You're always taking the worst of it when you're taking a draw; you know that you're always the underdog when you call a bet to draw to your hand.

For example, say that the board comes 2-3-10 and you have stood a little raise before the flop with 4-5 in a back position. Somebody makes a bet at you. I would never flat call with this drawing hand against a bet. I would either raise him right on the flop to try to blow him out of the pot, or throw away the hand. Why? Because if you don't make the draw on the first card off, he's going to come after you again and then you will have to dump your hand. With these types of connectors, your decision always comes *on the flop.*

Now suppose that you hold this same 4-5 and there are several people in the pot. The original bettor bets at the pot, someone calls, and then it's up to you. What do you do? Nothing has changed. If you make a play at the pot (raise) and blow both of them off, you will just win double money. But you're taking the chance of getting called, and then you will have nothing. That is why I either throw away the hand, or make the raise.

If Player A bets and Player B calls, what do I have with the 4-5 on the 2-3-10 flop? I have eight outs twice if my cards are still in the deck—if neither of them is holding two aces or two sixes. But I am not looking to get pot odds in a no-limit tournament. Anytime you make a play in a tournament and get beaten for all of your chips, you're out of the tournament. Although this thought always has to be in the back of your mind, it shouldn't be a fear factor. If you have fear in no-limit hold'em, you'd better not play the game.

Now suppose that you have J-10 in your hand and the flop comes 8-9-2. There is some strength in this hand: You have two overcards and the top straight draw. This is the type of overlay situation that you are looking for on your drawing hands. But the other question to consider if the board comes nine-high is, "Do I have two overs and a straight draw?" In an unraised pot, your opponent might have a J-9 or a 10-9 and then you both have only one overcard.

Tom gives this example of another suited connecting hand when the blinds are $25-$50 in the early stages of a tournament: "You are in sixth position with the 8♣ 9♣, and two limpers are in the pot. If you don't think that you will be raised, you can call with this hand. This example illustrates my two-limper rule in limit hold'em, which also applies somewhat in no-limit play.

If you limp with this hand in limit hold'em, and the pot is raised only one unit, you can call the raise; but in no-limit, if someone puts in a pot-sized raise before the flop, you dump the hand when you are out of position. If you are only slightly out of position in no-limit, say the sixth spot, and no one raises the pot, you can limp with the hand." This is a situation where "feel" comes into the game.

DANGER HANDS

If there is any raising before the pot, hands such as K-J, Q-10, and K-Q can be dangerous to play. You will get in far less trouble playing a 9-8 than you will a Q-J, because it is easier to get away from the drawing hand. A-10 and A-J also can be dangerous, because players often will slip into an unraised pot with A-K or A-Q.

The question is, "What do you have if you flop something to one of these hands?" Of course, it is far better to flop your second pair than your top pair, if your second-rank card is the highest card on the flop; but even then you could be in trouble. For example, if you play the Q-J and flop jacks, you are in kicker trouble.

These types of hands require the most careful decisions and the most skill. I might play these kinds of hands if I can open the pot with them— if I'm on the button in an unopened pot, for example—but I don't play them if I can only call with them, even from a late position.

Say that you have K-J and it is passed to you on the button ... then you might play this hand. It depends on who is left in the pot: The more timid the players, the more likely I will be to raise, but the more aggressive the players, the more likely I will be to just flat call. Some aggressive players don't respect any type of raise, and although they may figure that you have a better hand than they have, they're not going to give it up, and they may be able to outflop you.

In a no-limit tournament, I won't even venture into the pot from the first five positions with A-Q if it's early in the tournament. It's different when you're playing short-handed. But early in the tournament with a full table, I won't play an A-Q. If somebody raises, what do you do with this hand?

PLAYING THE BLINDS

Tom often will protect his blind. He tells a story about a time when he got broke in the big blind making a judgment call. "I was in the big blind in a no-limit tournament at the Queens Classic with A-9 offsuit and Thomas Chung was in the small blind. The action was passed to Brent Carter, who raised on the button. Carter didn't have to have a hand to raise; he had been playing a lot of pots and had a big pile of chips in front of him. With only a fraction of the bet in front of him, Chung called all-in from the small blind.

I knew that Chung was ready to make a stand with anything. so I thought that I had a reasonable chance of having the best hand in this situation. I overcalled for all of my chips, making the side pot far larger than the main pot. Carter was holding J-9 offsuit and spiked a jack on fourth street to beat me. Chung took the main pot with pocket aces."

Dana Smith, who was sweating Tom during the tournament, remarked that since Tom was low on chips and had enough to meet the small blind with some chips left over, he could have mucked the hand and then waited for the button. But his decision in this case was correct. He was playing the players and knew that Carter, with a ton of chips in front of him, didn't necessarily have to be holding a hand to make the raise. Also, if Chung had had enough chips to call the full raise, Tom would have thrown the hand away, because he would have been more afraid of Chung's call than of Carter's raise. The only way that you can avoid these types of situations is by never making those kinds of calls, but it is exactly this kind of call that separates the men from the boys in no-limit hold'em.

Here is another example from tournament play. A man raised in the small blind and I was in the big blind with A-K. He made a decent raise, but I moved in on him. He did not hesitate to call me. He went into the pot with a 6-3 offsuit and won the pot with a pair of sixes. When the hand was all over, he said, "I knew you didn't have anything." That was the most ridiculous statement I have ever heard in my life—he knew that *I* didn't have anything, but *he* had a six-high! I didn't mind losing the pot as much as I did hearing that statement.

PICKING UP THE BLINDS

Although the blinds are vulnerable positions, you can pick up a lot of blinds late in a tournament, especially from the button. If you don't have at least a semi-good hand in the blind, you have no business calling bets with it.

Say that someone raises the blind, and you have a J-8 or something like that. You might think to yourself, "Well, he's just trying to pick up my blind, so maybe I'll call him and hit the flop and pick him off." Ninety percent of the time, you'll be taking the worst of it. It's tough not to defend the blinds, especially if a very aggressive player is on the button, but you have to give up those types of hands.

In a different scenario, suppose that you have a K-Q in the big blind in a shorthanded game, an aggressive player raises from the button, and the little blind doesn't call. Now, you might have a shot. In this case, I might even reraise. At other times, the button might be raising with A-rag and have me beaten. You have to make a decision in these situations.

DEFENDING THE BLIND

There is nothing wrong with defending your blind with K-J or K-Q against a guy who always raises on the button in a shorthanded game. But a lot of players will always defend their blinds against a small raise if they already have a decent blind in the pot. If an aggressive player like Phil Hellmuth thinks that nobody will play back at him from the blinds, he will attack every time. But I will play back at these types of players, sometimes without a hand, and force them to be more careful about raising my blind. They don't know when I'm going to do it because *I* don't know when I'm going to do it.

I might let them take my blind two or three times and then come back over the top of them. This play does two things: It scares the pants off of them, and because the pot has been raised, you have all the money back that they have stolen from you in the other pots. You can lose three steals in a row, and then get all of your money back, plus a little, on their fourth steal attempt. When you try this steal-back, you want to make a big enough raise so that you can win the pot without seeing a flop. The message that you are sending them is, "My blind is not yours all of the time."

There also are players who will defend their blinds against aggressive button players because they get sick and tired of being run over, or their pride gets insulted, but you don't want to let your ego play your hand. If you're in the blind with an aggressive player who often raises on the button, you need to be very careful about what you call the raise with. Set your standards pretty high, especially in a full ring.

GETTING TO THE FINAL TABLE

The final table is composed of nine players, six of whom play on the final day for television. Usually, all nine are good players, and sometimes, there will be a player who has been very lucky over a period of time. Most often, they all will be world-class players. At the final table in the WSOP, the antes are usually $1,000 and the blinds are $10,000 and $20,000. (The blinds have gotten up to as high as $25,000-$50,000.)

Every time you play a pot, your whole idea in playing it is to get to the final table. Every time that you have to make a decision (for example, about calling a bet), you should be thinking to yourself, "If I call this bet and I'm wrong, I won't be getting to the final table." With this thinking always in your mind, all of the marginal hands that you are dealt should be very easy to throw away. It's different when you know that it's not a marginal decision — it's a pot that you have to call. But like I said earlier, in no-limit hold'em, being a caller means that you are setting up somebody to call. You always want to be the bettor; you don't want to be the caller unless you are setting a man up.

Suppose that there are three tables left. At this point, it's how you play your stack that counts. Let everybody else knock people out. Don't be too aggressive. You don't have to knock every player out yourself; let them do that to themselves. Increase your chips as you go along if you can, but just be satisfied to get there. You know that if you get to the last table, you have a chance to win—but you have no chance of winning unless you get to the final table. This should be the thing that you are thinking about all the time, not "Can I get to the money? Can I get to 27th place?" Always keep the big picture in mind—winning the tournament—not inching up the ladder. This is why I never have been happy with third or second, although I've won second and third money lots of times. My picture is always *first place*, and it always will be.

When I get to the final table, my goal is to win it, not to just move up through the ranks. A very easy scenario at the final table is to let everybody knock everybody else out, and then you knock out the final player. That's the best strategy, unless some hands come along. So, you just play premium hands. If you have a short stack, you have to make a stand somewhere along the line, so you pick the best hand that you think you're going to get and you play it.

The optimal situation, of course, is that you knock every single player out at the final table, but remember that any time you are all-in, you have to win that pot or you're gone. This seems like the simplest concept in the world, but you have to keep it in the back of your mind all the time: "Any time that I go all-in, I have to win the pot." This is true of the first day through the fourth day.

I've played in a lot of tournaments at a lot of limits where I was never all-in at any time during the tournament. And that's nice, really nice. There have been other tournaments in which I have been all-in numerous times, usually by choice—by *moving* all-in, not *calling* all-in.

SIZING UP THE OPPOSITION

At the final table, you can size up who is trying to win the tournament and who is trying to just finish high. You usually can tell by the way they're playing. If a player is just trying to last, you can attack him, take his big blinds away from him. This type of player is waiting for others to get knocked out so he can slip into a higher position. You'll find these types in every tournament, especially the WSOP. A lot of them are just trying to make any kind of money finish and get their names in the brochure. They have given up the big picture, and any chance of winning.

So, I want to take advantage of these types of players, wait for some players to get knocked out, and only play top hands. I want to get into the top three myself, but I'm not going to get there by becoming passive.

Very few flops are seen at the final table; there are more non-flops than anything else. There are virtually no multiway pots, no limpers, no three-way pots. The most unusual pot came up in 1989, the year that Phil Hellmuth won it, when it was four-handed at the final table. At this key time in the tournament, two players were eliminated in a three-way pot, which is almost unheard of in World Series final action. When the pot is contested, 95 percent of the time it's head-up action.

WHEN YOU GET INTO THE MONEY

Once you get into the money, the final twenty-seven players, things change and the action moves much faster right away. Players start playing more hands, hands that they wouldn't have played before they got into the money. People are taking more chances and a lot more gambling is going on. Why do they do this? Because they have at least gotten their money back, and a lot of them are short-stacked and begin taking chances that they wouldn't take earlier in the tournament. This is when you can sit back with your big stack and watch them knock each other off. The idea is to play good poker. Where the other guys are all firing, you're playing solid.

The action slows down again when it gets down to 11 or 12 players. This is when I *don't* slow down. This is when I open up, going against the stream. I want to gather chips in this situation, just like I do when it gets down to five players, and so I open up because other players are slowing down. There are places where you can really add to your chip count, going against the ebb and flow. So, when the other guys are playing loose-aggressive at the third table, you're playing solid. And when they're playing solid in the twelfth through ninth spots, you're playing more aggressively. When I talk about being aggressive, I'm not talking about being a fool, either. There's a big difference between the two.

In this very late stage, you virtually never limp in. Once you're headed for the final table, from about the third table on, it is rare that anyone limps. I am more afraid of somebody limping at the final table than I am if he had raised. A ton of bells start going off in my head, saying "Watch out! Watch out!"

Someone very easily could be setting a trap. Of course, he could just be limping in because he thinks that's the best thing to do, but you don't want to take a shot from one of these guys.

Again, you have to know your players and avoid making any bonehead plays. If you haven't been observing your opponents so that you know how they play, you don't deserve to be at the final table.

6

HOW TO PRACTICE FOR WINNING THE WORLD SERIES OF POKER

GETTING EXPERIENCE

There are two major ways to practice for the big no-limit tournaments: Play in the small tournaments, the $200 and $300 buy-in events, and play the one-table satellites for the big tournaments. Although you don't get as many chips to start with as you do in the WSOP events, playing in these smaller tournaments is a good way to learn how to play tournament poker.

The experience that you will get is far superior than playing in satellites. Just remember that you usually are playing against people who are on your same skill level, or possibly just a bit above you; but you seldom are playing the top players.

Because you can beat someone at your level of skill doesn't mean that you are a world beater. You have to be able to beat the people on the top level.

SMALL TOURNAMENTS

A lot of cardrooms sponsor smaller buy-in no-limit tournaments in which you can win a seat for the WSOP $10,000 main event. I suggest that you play in these tournaments to get experience in playing the WSOP structure, in which you have a lot of chips to start with. I use exactly the same method of play in $500 tournaments that I do in $5,000 or $10,000 tournaments.

The element that makes the WSOP's final event so different from the lesser buy-in tournaments is that you start with $10,000 in chips. Obviously, more play is possible when you begin with $10,000 in chips than when you start with only $500 in chips.

ONE-TABLE SATELLITES

To get experience playing against top players, try the one-table satellites, because a lot of the best players use the one-tables to make extra money. In the one-table satellites for a big tournament, you can learn a lot about how players play, how they treat situations, and you have enough chips to maneuver around and play the game.

The entry fee for the $5,000 one-table satellites is $500; for the $10,000 big one, it is $1,000. Although that's a lot of money to pay for a satellite, you might learn a lot and end up making a lot of money in the long run.

One thing that I like about the one-table satellites for the big one is that you are given $2,000 in chips, which gives you some maneuverability. In the one-table satellites for the $5,000 and $10,000 tournaments, you have more chips to start with, and the blinds start out smaller in relation to the size of the chips in play. Also, the rounds are 20 minutes (rather than fifteen minutes), giving more advantage to the better players.

When I sit down at a one-table satellite for one of the big tournaments, I usually look around the table to see who is playing. Invariably, I can predict two out of the final three players—the players that I think have a chance of getting there and the ones that I believe will make too many mistakes to win unless the cards run over them.

Of course, some upsets happen in satellites. I have seen a table full of experts with only two novices in the game, and the novices got head up at the end. But in that case, they drew out a few times. So, your best bet for getting practice is playing the smaller no-limit hold'em tournaments, and the one-table satellites for the larger tournaments.

SUPERSATELLITES

The supersatellites, in which you get $200 in chips, are much tougher to win because they become move-in games. This is why I don't think that supersatellites are as good a learning experience as the one-tables or the smaller tournaments. But don't get me wrong: I'm all for supersatellites. Winning one of them may be the only way that some people have of getting into the big tournaments. In fact, more than 100 players win their entries into the WSOP in the supersatellites.

One good rule that the WSOP has put in is that the winner must play in the tournament for which he wins his first supersatellite. If he wins more than one, he can sell the subsequent seats that he wins.

Remember, too, that you don't have to *win* a supersatellite to get a seat in the big tournament. Four seats for the WSOP usually are given out at each of the big satellites at Binion's Horseshoe, so you only need to place in the top four. As soon as the satellite is played down to four people, the seats are awarded and the game is over. You don't need to prove your ability to win, you just need to prove that you can get to the final four. (In a one-table satellite, you play down to the final winner, unless you make a deal on the end.)

The purpose of playing satellites is to get into a tournament cheaply, not to learn poker, although a lot of people like to play the supersatellites so that they can get experience playing against top players. Satellites for big tournaments also can be a very good way of making pocket cash.

One year at the Hall of Fame tournament, I played in six supersatellites and won a seat in four of them. Then I played in six one-table satellites and won a seat in four of those too, so the satellites turned out to be profitable ventures for me.

YOUR BEST VALUE

More money is given away in tournaments than anybody ever thought of giving away in side games. This is the main reason why your best value in a tournament is the tournament itself, not the side games, especially at World Series time.

A lot of weak players enter the WSOP events, either by winning a satellite or by ponying up $2,000 and more. There is so much dead money in tournaments that good players have a huge overlay, especially in pot-limit and no-limit games, because the skill factor is so much higher in these games than it is in limit hold'em.

For example, when 145 people signed up for the final

event in 1985, we looked over the list of players and said, "Well, there are 75 who have no chance at all; there might be thirty-five players who can go all the way to the third day; there are about twenty-five who can make the final table; and maybe ten of those twenty-five actually could win it." This is what I mean by "dead money."

One of the changes that has increased attendance at the WSOP, especially in the championship event, is making players play the tournament for which they win their first supersatellite. This requirement has swelled attendance more than any other single factor.

All of the top players love having larger fields, because a lot of people who are capable of winning a satellite seldom win a major tournament, because they are not able to put together a game for two to four days. They may play very well during the first day, but they cannot do it over the long haul because their skill level just isn't high enough. Although the fields are even larger in limit hold'em, a lot more players know how to play the game well, so there are far fewer "sacrificial lambs" than there are in no-limit.

Of course, Tom and I both hope that you have increased your skill level through studying this book to the point that we will all meet in the winners circle one day soon.

SATELLITE STRATEGY

I have heard a lot of people suggest that playing satellites is a good way for limit hold'em players to learn how to play no-limit. I think that is a fallacy. In a satellite, you begin with very few chips.

If you're playing in a $10,000 or $5,000 satellite, you start with only $200-to-$500 in chips. With so few chips, it is basically a move-in game with all the play taken out of it. Because the antes go up every fifteen minutes or so, you usually move your chips all in when you get a hand that you like, whereas in a ring game, you try to use your abilities and play out a pot.

At the Golden Nugget, I once played in a $10,000 satellite in which five people moved in their entire stacks ($2,000) on the first hand. So after the very first hand, one player had $10,000 and nobody else had more than $2,000. He didn't win it; in fact, he didn't even come in second!

The way to play satellites is to sit back and let the other players knock each other out. Wait for a big hand. You get $300 in chips in a no-limit $500 satellite. The beginning blinds are $5-$15 with no ante. In a ten-handed game, it costs you $20 every round (every ten hands) for the first fifteen minutes. Then the blinds rise to $10-$25, so every round costs you $40 during the next fifteen minutes. During the first half-hour, you should be able to pick up at least one hand. But a lot of players are playing 8-6, A-7 (any ace), K-Q, or any two suited cards, and they're getting busted with those types of hands.

By waiting patiently for a hand, you may suddenly find yourself down to four-handed play, and you don't have many chips.

A lot of players panic at this point because they are short-stacked and the other players have a lot of chips. But the blind structure remains the same, and you can pick up a couple of hands and get back in the ball game if you play correctly. So, the way to play satellites is to let players knock out each other and then you take on the survivors. When it gets down to the playing part, you take them off at the end. You get one hand, get back in the ball game, and then you simply outplay them. You start attacking them when it gets down to three or four players. I have won a lot of satellites using this strategy.

Since there is never an ante in satellites, the only difference in playing no-limit and pot-limit satellites is that in pot-limit, you can only bet the size of the pot. You play the same strategy in each type of game. If you play this strategy, by the time you do your real playing in the later stages of a pot-limit satellite, the blinds are so high, and there are so many chips at stake, that it is almost like playing no-limit.

Junior Prejean used to bet on me in satellites. If they were laying 3-to-1 on me winning a no-limit satellite, he would bet on me. (The real odds actually were 9-to-1.) One time, we were in a $10,000 satellite and Gary Slade, who's a big gambler and has been around for a few years, said that he would lay 7-to-1 that I couldn't win the satellite. Herb Bronstein came over from one game, and John Bonetti came over from another game, and I bet on myself. At 7-to-1, I would take those odds any day. The side bets got up to at least $10,000. It only cost $1,000 to play the satellite, but Slade had $10,000 bet on it at 7-to-1.

At that rate, he stood to lose some real money. It got down to Slade and me, I had the lead, and he settled out for 3.5-to-1. I won the satellite, and he lost about $10,500 on the deal and didn't even win the satellite.

A lot of deals go on in the satellites, but I am not a deal maker in either the satellites or the tournaments, although I can see why a lot of people make deals. In forty-three tournament victories, I have made five deals.

A lot of times when you make deals, it takes the edge off your play. You don't play the same way that you would without a deal. Actually, I don't believe that deal making should be allowed in tournaments. Most players know that I usually won't make a deal and so, even when it comes down to three-handed, they don't offer to make a deal. I always believe that if I have enough skill to get that far, I have enough skill to go the rest of the distance. Tom likes to make deals, and that is another way to look at things.

Before I had backers, I would swap pieces of myself with other people. My wife and I figured out that I had swapped out $337,000 and had collected back $26,000. We decided that I should stop doing that.

The year that Berry Johnston won the WSOP, I was going to swap five percent of myself with five or six players. So I went to Berry and Mike Hart and they said that they thought they would like to swap, but they couldn't make a commitment until the day of the tournament. In the meantime, I went to Johnny Chan and Chip Reese and a few of the other top players and swapped twenty-five percent of myself. The morning of the Big One, both Berry and Mike came to me and said yes, let's swap. But by then I had already swapped out twenty-five percent of myself and I turned them down.

They ran one-two in the tournament! I would have gotten back over $50,000 on the deal. *C'est la vie.*

REBUY TOURNAMENTS

You can rebuy during the first three hours in most rebuy tournaments at the lower levels. The blinds increase during these three hours. If you're playing in a $500 tournament, and all that you can rebuy is $500, once the antes get up to $25-$50, then it really isn't feasible to rebuy for $500 when the antes can eat you alive. I think that the rebuy setup that Amarillo Slim once used is better. In his rebuy tournament, the first rebuy was for $200; the second rebuy was $500; and all of the subsequent rebuys were $1,000. This was a good structure because the rebuy always gave you enough money to play at the higher limits.

Jack McClelland has had quite an influence on rebuy tournaments at the WSOP and the other tournaments that he coordinates. It was his brainchild to allow rebuys to continue for three hours; in other tournaments, that usually is not the case. I like having rebuys for three hours because it gets more money into the tournament.

In McClelland's tournaments, you can rebuy any number of times during the first three hours, and the only requirement is that you have less than the amount of chips that you started with (less than $1,000 in a $1,000 tournament, for example). Then, you can take a double add-on at the end of the rebuy period if you have less than what you bought in for. For players who want to continue playing, the double add-on is a good idea. You have to decide what the tournament is worth to you, how much you can win for the amount of money that it's costing you.

You should get a pretty big percentage of return on your investment in a tournament—that's what tournaments are all about. You want to get a good overlay on your money. If the win end of the tournament isn't at least fifty times the amount of money that you have put in, it really isn't a good tournament for you. So, if you pay $1,000 to enter a tournament, you want to be able to win $50,000. Actually, I think that you should be able to win more than fifty times your investment, but the only tournament that is structured so that you do that is the WSOP.

I especially like the rebuy and add-on options for no-limit tournaments because no-limit is the only type of game that you can get broke on in one hand. It can happen in pot-limit, but it usually doesn't happen at the lower levels, whereas in no-limit you can be gone at any time.

POST-TOURNAMENT STRESS

The worst feeling that you can ever have in tournament poker is when you have made the right move or the right call, you get all of your money in there, and then somebody draws out on you. You've made the right decision but you got the wrong result. You always feel lousy when you get knocked out late in a tournament.

Tom says that he suffers burnout several times a year, especially right after the WSOP. "I'm just worthless for several days after the Series," he said, "and so I make a complete change of pace and do something other than play poker."

Me, I go play golf for five or six days in a row. I've even played in 36-degree weather at home in Texas!

There definitely is a tournament stress factor while you're playing a tournament, and it takes a while to come down from that afterward. If you're not drained at the end of each day at the tournament, you're not giving your best effort. If you're not coming home mentally and physically worn out, you haven't played your best game. In football, you can give fifty percent and be whacked out, but unless you've giving 100 percent in poker, you haven't done your best. People have told me that they can't sleep after winning a tournament — I sleep so well, it's unbelievable. I go right to sleep, because I'm whacked out. If you can't sleep, I think it's because you haven't given your all.

Playing a tournament for three weeks is like working hard at a job for three months. Tom says that it's like being on an adrenaline rush; that's what keeps him going. It is though his immune system can resist anything during the competition but when the tournament is over, his system lets down and he gets sick. I suggest a total change of pace right after a big tournament. You need some time to recharge your batteries and get your mind in shape for the next big event.

WORLD CLASS NO-LIMIT HOLD'EM PLAYERS

I think that one of the best no-limit players, day to day, is Bobby Hoff. Jack Straus and a lot of the players who were in Bobby's category are gone now. He knows where he's at better than most players do, and he's an aggressive player who never slows down. If I had to pick one man to put my money on in a head-up match, it would be Bobby Hoff.

Carl McKelvey from Texas is a very good ring player. Although he is not a tournament specialist, he has both won and finished high in no-limit tournaments. He is an excellent no-limit hold'em player who has good judgment, is solid, can loosen up, and has more than one speed.

Big Bill O'Connor also is an excellent player and Bill Duarte, the one we call "Boston Billy," has turned into a very good player. And in his own style, John Bonetti is an excellent player because he gets there. When Stuey was Stuey, Stu Ungar was on the top of my list.

But the smartest card player I've ever played cards against, and the smartest man that I've ever met, is Lyle Berman. He plays against Doyle and Chip and the other legends in side games, and he gets the cash more times than he doesn't. If you've ever talked poker with him, you've found out that he's an encyclopedia of poker; he knows all the different angles and he has everything in his head. Here's a man who is running a big corporation who shouldn't be able to do all these things on the side. He doesn't play that often, but when he plays, and they're playing high, there is no one better than him in any game that he plays, not only no-limit hold'em.

Chip Reese is the best all-around player alive. He's proven that over the years and everybody agrees that he's the best. When he sets his mind to it, Doyle can play hold'em and most of the other games with anybody alive. And nobody could touch Johnny Chan in the tournaments for quite a few years. He set up his hands and played the players perfectly. These are all top players.

A man from Dallas named Bill Bonds, who doesn't play very often in tournaments, played in the toughest games in the nation and was the most consistent winner in the game year after year after year. A lot of people have never heard of Bill, but he's a top hold'em player. And I always give credit to Jim Ashey, the man we called "Little

Red." He was a great player. Steve Lott also is an excellent player.

There also are proven tournament players. Tom is a proven player himself, and I rate him better at limit hold'em than no-limit. Berry Johnston is very good in anything that he plays. He had to move to Vegas because he broke Oklahoma City—of all the gamblers there, he had all the money. I kid him about it, telling him that now he's working on Las Vegas. Dan Harrington, and Russ Hamilton are very good players: Each of them has won the World Series.

Among the young crew that I rate high are Phil Hellmuth, Huck Seed, Erik Seidel and Howard Lederer. Phil is a wonderful tournament player, especially when he gets some chips in a tournament and when he gives other players a little bit of credit. In a different way, Howard is every bit as good a player as Phil. The players like Bobby Hoff, Carl McKelvey, and Bill O'Connor have a lot more experience at no-limit hold'em than the young players. If all of these players played in a ring game together, I believe that Hoff, McKelvey, and O'Connor would get the money more times than the other players on my list, although Howard plays solid enough and has enough gears that he would be more likely to get the money over the other young players.

Tom puts me on his list of top no-limit players, and I appreciate his comments. "What sets T.J. apart is his memory of how people play in different situations, his knowledge of their tells," he said. "And T.J. is willing to give his opponents some respect for their playing ability. He doesn't underrate his opponents as often as other top players do." Tom describes my style as playing a very patient, controlled game, looking for spots, playing the players, just waiting for an opening.

"You're like a snake hiding under a rock, ready to strike when your opponents make mistakes," Dana Smith told me. But actually, I'm more like a well-coiled cobra. Of course, I remember way back when Terry Rogers was booking the World Series of Poker and sending his odds over to England. For some reason, he made me the big favorite one year. He started me off at 35-to-1 and when it got down to 15-to-1, he took me off the board. The "big favorite" went out on the first day that year!

Tom McEvoy, winner of the
1992 World Series of Poker limit Omaha Championship.
He is shown here playing high stakes with his partner

7

NO-LIMIT HOLD'EM PRACTICE HANDS

In this chapter, there are some practice hands. After looking at each hand, think about how you would play it. Then read the analysis that T. J. gives for the play of the hand and compare it with your ideas.

In each example, Player A is the first to act; Player B is the next to act; and Player C is last to act.

PRACTICE HAND 1

At a no-limit tournament table, Player A raised $1200 before the flop. Player B reraised $1200. Player C cold-called the reraise, and Player A called. Assume that you are Player B. Your hand is:

The flop comes:

SCENARIO ONE

Player A bets $8,000 on the flop. What is your best move?

I would have folded this hand before the flop if I had been Player B. But if you decide to play the hand, you should either flat-call the $1200 to see what comes on the flop, or raise about four times that amount (if you have enough chips). You would put in a big enough raise to shut out the rest of the field so that you can play heads up against one opponent.

If you make a large raise, the original raiser...

(a) may throw his hand away and you will win the pot right there, or

(b) may call. In either case, your raise probably will freeze out the rest of the field.

But Player B didn't do that. He let Player C into the pot (who even cold called B's raise), so Player B has to give both Player C and Player A credit for having good hands.

Why would I throw the hand away when Player A bets $8,000 on the flop? For two reasons: First of all, Player A has either A-A, A-K, Q-Q, or A-Q. Or if he's a loose player, he could have two sevens in his hand. Since I have the K♠ in my hand, I don't put him on a spade draw. Secondly, since Player C cold-called behind me, he also could have flopped a set.

Therefore, I would fold the A-K.

SCENARIO TWO

Player A checks on the flop. What do you do? You also check.

SCENARIO THREE

Player A moves all-in on the flop. What is your best move? Pass.

ANALYSIS

Some of the key elements for analysis that are missing from this scenario are the number of players who are at the table; whether this hand comes up in the early, middle, or late stage of the tournament; and how much you know about your opponents.

Because you have been studying the game while you were playing, you should know which players will raise or reraise with A-J or A-Q, and which players will not raise unless they have aces or kings. If your opponent is the type of player who won't raise with a weak hand, you don't have anything with the A-K, so why not get rid of it?

Now, suppose that you have $2,500 in front of you, and you bring it in for $1,500. Then somebody reraises behind you. You are pot-committed and you go on with the play because you have more than one-half of your chips already in the pot. An experienced player often will pot-commit himself by putting in most of his chips when he raises because he knows that if he gets reraised, he will automatically go for the rest of it. A less experienced player might think that he can blow the raiser off the hand by reraising. He mistakenly believes that the raiser will save that extra $500 or $1,000 that he has left.

What the inexperienced reraiser doesn't realize is that the only reason that the raiser has pot-committed himself is so that he cannot get away from the hand. ♠

PRACTICE HAND 2

This time, let's fill in some of the missing elements from Practice Hand One. You are playing in a $1,000 buy-in tournament. It is in the middle stage of the tournament and you are playing at a full table.

Player A raises $1,200 before the flop. You are Player B sitting in fifth position with four players behind you. You reraise $4,800. Player C cold calls the reraise for $6,000, and Player A calls.

You hold the same hand that you had in Practice Hand One:

The flop comes:

SCENARIO ONE

Player A checks on the flop. What is your best move? You are in a quandary. You have top pair and the nut flush draw, and there is $18,000 in the pot. This could be the perfect trap hand, but you have to play it, so you move in with all of your chips. If you're up against a set, of course, you can't beat it, but still, you're drawing to the nut flush.

It doesn't matter what Player C does; you're playing the hand.

SCENARIO TWO

Player A bets. What do you do? Again, you move all-in. You can't hope for a better flop, unless it had come A-A-K. This is a flop that you have to play. ♠

PRACTICE HAND 3

Once again, you have been dealt Big Slick. The tournament conditions and pre-flop action are the same as in Practice Hand Two.

Your hand is:

This time, the flop comes:

SCENARIO ONE

Player A bets. Your observation has told you that Player A is a pretty good player. What do you do with your A-K? You pass. A lot of times, good players will move with a big hand in the hope that you will play back at them.

Since I know that Player A is a strong player, I would throw the hand away.

SCENARIO TWO

Player A checks. Now what do you do? If Player A checks, you check. Then, if Player C bets, you throw the hand away.

ANALYSIS

Tossing your hand is tough to do because you have a lot of money in the pot. But why give up the tournament for this one hand? The A-K is a perfect trap hand, unless you're playing at a shorthanded table and then it becomes a powerful hand. If you're playing against five or fewer players, A-K is a strong hand, but if you're in a full ring, there are a lot of scenarios when Big Slick amounts to nothing. You want to avoid any traps that you can get into with it.

Two queens is a decent raising hand, one that a lot of players will stand a reraise with. (I won't stand a reraise with the hand, but many players will.) Therefore, given this flop, there is a good chance that either Player A or Player C has flopped quad queens—or a full house if either one is holding an A-Q.

People think that Big Slick is such a big-big hand, but it isn't. Two deuces is a better hand than A-K. In a computer run of 100,000 hands, two deuces will win more often than A-K in heads-up situations played to a showdown. ♠

PRACTICE HAND 4

You have Big Slick, the same hand that you held in the last three Practice Hands:

The flop comes with three baby cards:

SCENARIO ONE

Player A bets. What do you do? You throw your hand away. Why? Because you have nothing.

In no-limit hold'em, you never chase.

SCENARIO TWO

Player A checks. You also check.

SCENARIO THREE

Player A checks. You check. Player C bets. You fold, no matter what Player A does after Player C bets. Again, you never chase with A-K in no-limit hold'em.

ANALYSIS

Remember that Player C has cold called a reraise before the flop and is yet to act after you. It's fairly certain that he can beat a pair of deuces, fours, or sevens — and your A-K can't beat any of those pairs. So, that is another reason why you dump your A-K if he bets. ♠

PRACTICE HAND 5

Now let's look at several scenarios that demonstrate how you might play pocket aces from early position when you are the first player in the pot.

SCENARIO ONE

You are Player A sitting in early position and have been dealt:

You limp into the pot. The player next to the button raises. The button and both of the blinds fold. You decide to just call.

The flop comes:

Now what do you do? Since you have set things up to slow-play your hand, you check. Player B bets. What's your play?

You just flat-call.

Now, suppose the turn card is the 2♠:

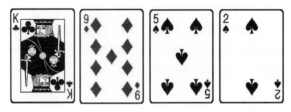

You check. Player B puts in a big bet. What do you do? You raise, knowing that there's a good chance that you'll get played with if Player B has something like A-K or a pocket pair such as queens or jacks. Player B calls.

The river card is another deuce:

You bet. Player B calls and shows A♠ K♠. He had top pair with the nut flush draw on the turn.

ANALYSIS

Because you limped, he probably thought that he had the best hand by a long shot, or at the worst, a tie. He didn't put you on a set, and most players wouldn't even consider that you might have two aces. This is the perfect scenario for slowplaying pocket aces and getting full value from them. It is one way of trapping your opponent.

Now let's look at a different style of slow-playing aces from early position.

SCENARIO TWO

You are Player A. This time you raise from early position with your pocket aces. Player B reraises. What do you do? You flat call.

The board comes the same as Scenario One:

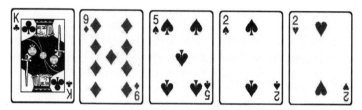

What do you do? Lead at the pot with a standard bet.

ANALYSIS

When the flop comes K-9-5, you are thinking, "How can I get the most out of this pot? If I lead, Player B probably will raise if he has A-K." So, you lead at the pot with a standard bet—you don't want him to fold so you don't make a huge bet. You want to bet the amount that you believe he will call if he has any kind of hand.

Whether he calls or raises, you have him trapped (unless, of course, he has pocket kings, in which case you're the one who is trapped). You lead at this hand all the way through—his pre-flop reraise and call on the flop tell you that he is pot-committed. In this situation, your pre-flop raise built a decent pot for you to win.

SCENARIO THREE

You are Player A. You raise from early position with:

Player B reraises. Player C cold-calls the reraise. Now what do you do? Bet all in.

ANALYSIS

In this situation, you know that Player C has a big hand, probably K-K or Q-Q, so you go over the top with an all-in bet. There's plenty of money in the pot already, so you simply move on it. You hope for a call, but even if neither Player B nor Player C calls, you still have won a decent pot.

SCENARIO FOUR

Now suppose you reraise Player C's raise, Player B folds, and Player C calls your reraise. The flop comes the same as in Scenarios One and Two. How do you play the hand?

You have two options: You either lead at it all the way, or you just move in on the flop. You want to get paid off on your aces, but even if Player C does not call, you've still won a big pot with your aggressive play of pocket aces from up front. ♠

PRACTICE HAND 6

You are sitting in a middle position with:

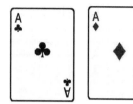

Suppose you're in a real action game, a player limps, you limp, two or three other players also limp, and then a guy who has been raising every pot puts in a raise. What do you do? Whenever the pot is opened or raised in the first three seats, you have two options:

(1) You can reraise, or

(2) You can play "second-hand low."

In this situation, you have set things up to play second-hand low. You know that you have a real action player behind you, so when somebody leads into the pot in front of you, you just call. You suspect that the original limper might also have a big hand, so you're setting the stage to raise both the limper and the action player.

The first player in the pot might have a decent hand, but you have aces. Player A or the raiser might reraise the pot and now you have a big pot to win before the flop. So if you reraise the pot right there, they might figure that you are just trying to pick up the pot, or that you have an A-K or something like that. They hardly ever put you on aces when you play second-hand low. You're trying to trap everybody. You want to make them pay to try to draw out on your aces.

Now let's take a look at another scenario when you're holding aces in a middle position.

SCENARIO ONE

You are in middle position holding A♠ A♣. You raised the pot before the flop and you were called by Player B on the button and Player C in the big blind.

The flop comes:

You make a standard bet in the hope of getting called by A-Q, K-Q, Q-J, Q-10, a nine with a big kicker, or J-10 (straight draw), or someone with a diamond draw. You could get beaten by these drawing hands or by the pair hands if they double-pair with their kicker. But in all of these scenarios, you still are the favorite on the flop. The only drawing hand that you could face that is favored over your aces would be the J♦ 10♦, and even that hand is only slightly favored.

The fourth street card is the 5♥.

On the turn you should make sure that you bet enough to put pressure on your opponents. You want to force them to make a decision as to whether they want to commit a lot of money to this pot. Obviously you are a good favorite over all the hands that we have mentioned.

The 2♥ comes at the river.

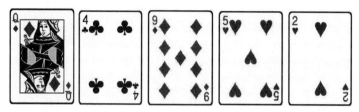

At the river, if anyone has stayed in the hand, I would empty out (bet all my chips) hoping to get called. The way that the hand has been played should indicate that A-A is still the best hand. In this scenario, I did not forget about the possibility that an opponent might have flopped a set. But because of the straight and flush possibilities on board, I am sure that if anyone had flopped a set, he would have moved on the flop, or certainly on fourth street.

SCENARIO TWO

Before the flop, one player limps in from an early position. You know from his previous play that he could be holding anything. You are the next to act. Your hand is A♣ A♦. You decide to just call. The button, the small blind and the big blind also flat-call.

The flop comes:

The two blinds and the early limper check. What do you do?

You also check. The button bets, the two blinds fold, and the original limper calls. Obviously you don't know exactly what hands the button and the limper have, but you do know that you have the best possible hand now. Therefore you have two choices:

(a) Flat-call knowing that you have disguised the strength of your hand, in the hope of winning a huge pot on fourth or fifth street.

(b) Raise the pot on the flop so as not to give any free cards. Let's take a look at two possible scenarios that illustrate these two options.

FLAT CALL ON THE FLOP

Along with the early-position limper, you flat-called the button's bet on the flop. The turn card is the 10♣.

Now you have them where you want them, but how do you get the most value from your hand? If the limper checks, lead at the pot with a decent bet in the hope of either getting raised and/or called by either or both of your opponents. Now if either player raises, he has committed himself to the pot. In that case, you go on the offensive and move all in. You know that there is a very good chance that at least one of them is on a big draw, has flopped a set, or has top two pair.

Now, suppose one of them calls your all-in bet and the river comes:

You're in clover! But what if either or both opponents just flat-call on the turn? In that case, on fifth street when you know that you have the nuts, you bet the amount that you think they will call. You don't move in because you don't want them to throw their hands away, you simply want to get full value from your aces.

The difference between good players and average players is that a good player always does whatever it takes to get full value from a hand.

RAISE ON THE FLOP

Now suppose that you choose to raise the pot right on the flop so as not to give any free cards, but still with the hope that either or both opponent call. Understand that if either opponent calls the raise, his hand would have to be a set, top two pair, top and bottom pair, A-K or A-Q, a flush draw, or a pair with a flush draw. (In this case, if someone has a pair and a flush draw, he would have to have an ace and a flush draw.)

Let's say that both the limper and the button call your raise. Again, the board looks like this on fourth street:

The limper checks. What do you do? You make a big bet, in the hope of either winning the pot right there or getting called by either or both opponents.

Suppose the button calls and the limper folds. Again the 5♠ comes at the river. This time you are the first to act—what do you do?

It's time for the kill! You've put him on a big hand, so you shove in all your chips to find out just how important it is to him. Does life get much sweeter than this? ♠

PRACTICE HAND 7

Suppose you are player C and you are sitting in late position with:

How do you play your hand? Raise. It doesn't matter how many people are in the pot, you're going to raise. If someone has raised in front of you with a lot of players in the pot, you're going to reraise. You cannot give free cards very often in a tournament if you want to survive.

A lot of times, too, your opponents will discount the strength of a late-position raise and will play with you because they believe you're on a steal.

ANALYSIS

After everyone has passed to the button, you sometimes will see people limp with pocket aces, but I think that's a horrible play. The chances of someone raising from either of two blinds are slim since you have two of the four aces in the deck locked up. And if they don't raise, they're going to get free cards on the flop with any kind of hand and you will have no idea of where you are with your aces. Therefore I think that you definitely should raise with aces when you're in late position.

Make your standard raise if you're the first one in the pot, or if there's only one limper in front of you. But if more than one player already is in the pot, you should consider moving all in. Any time that you have pocket aces, you want someone to come after you with a reraise. Then your decision is whether to just flat-call and try to nail him after the flop, or move in immediately to try to win the pot right there. If you flat-call, there's always the danger that your opponent will outflop you. But when you're playing aces in no-limit poker, you're always trying to maximize your hand so you choose the strategy that will best serve that purpose. ♠

PRACTICE HAND 8

Suppose you are Player C and you are sitting in the small blind holding:

How do you play your hand? Raise. When you have aces in one of the blinds, it is more important to raise than it is in any other position.

Why?

Because after the flop, you always have to act first. You're in the weakest position at the start of the hand, so you need to play aces like you're supposed to play them and raise.

Now suppose everybody checks to the button. The button raises and the small blind folds. What do you do? In this situation you might try to trap him by just flat-calling the raise in the hope that something will come on the flop that hits him a little bit but hits you even better. The best scenario that you're hoping for is that your opponent has something like A-6.

PRACTICE HAND 9

You are playing in a $1,000 buy-in no-limit hold'em tournament in the middle stage. You are Player A, the first to act. You have been dealt:

How would you play the hand before the flop?

SCENARIO ONE

You might limp with the two kings from front position, hoping that someone will raise. If somebody behind you has pocket aces, the more power to him. If you run into aces, there's nothing you can do about it. The strategy behind limping with the kings is to let somebody raise you so that you can reraise and win the pot right there. If a player just calls, you still have the second-best hand that you can start with, and you're just hoping that no ace comes on the board.

The reason why two kings is so hard to play is because it seems that an ace so often comes on the flop when you have the kings.

SCENARIO TWO

Say that you limp with the kings, Player B raises, and Player C calls the raise. Then you reraise. More than likely, you will win the pot right there, unless either Player B or C has aces or queens. If either one of them reraises you, you're probably a gone goose. If Player B has aces, for example, he will move you all-in, but if he doesn't do that, there's a pretty good chance that you have the best hand. If Player C reraises, he would have to be a very good player to be playing "second hand low."

Second hand low is when somebody else brings it in, and you just call with the aces in the hope that somebody behind you will raise and drive the first bettor back into you so that you can get all of the money in before the flop. It takes a very good player to pull off this play, and you don't see it very often in tournaments.

Therefore, it is unlikely that Player C is using this strategy.

ANALYSIS

Two kings is the second-best pair you can be dealt, but it also is the most dangerous. Why? Because it is a very hard hand to get away from before the flop. Usually, if there is one raise, you're going to reraise with two kings. Of course, there is the chance that you will run into two aces, or a big ace, or even "any ace."

If somebody with an ace in his hand calls you, you're a goner if an ace comes on the flop.

Any time that the flop is raised and reraised before it gets to you in a tournament, I suggest that you dump your two kings. Even if you are wrong once in a while, you will save a lot of money in the long run. ♠

PRACTICE HAND 10

Now, let's take a look at a hand that came up during the first level of play at the $10,000 World Series of Poker tournament. I picked up these cards:

I made it $300 to go. Jay Heimowitz, who is an expert player, called. The flop came:

I bet $400 at the pot and Jay made a big raise of around $3,000. I didn't hesitate in throwing away the kings because I knew that he wouldn't be raising me with anything less than two aces or a set. Sure enough, he showed me pocket nines.

I knew that because of the caliber of player Jay is, he would not have stood a raise with a hand such as A-J; he must have had a pocket pair. The only pairs that I could have beaten on the flop were tens, jacks, or queens. When you're playing against a top player like Jay, he isn't moving in with two jacks, two queens, or even two kings.

I figured that he either had two aces or a set. He wouldn't have 10-8 or 8-6 for a straight draw. I lost $700 on the hand, but at least I wasn't knocked out.

Actually, this was the second time in a row that Jay had flopped top set against an overpair. On the hand just before this one came up, Tommy Grimes had two aces and brought it in for about $400. Jay called the bet. The flop came 10-7-2. Tommy bet $2,000 at the pot and Jay moved in. Tommy made the mistake of calling him. Jay had flopped top set, trip tens, and knocked Tommy out of the tournament.

ANALYSIS

How you play pocket kings against a rag flop depends, once again, on what you know about your opponents. If I were playing Joe Blow from Idaho, I might give him a little action on this hand, especially if I knew that he was a limit hold'em player. Limit players seem to think that when they have top pair with top kicker or an overpair in no-limit, they have the Holy City.

A player like Jay Heimowitz knows that I either have an overpair or am taking a shot with A-K or A-Q (since it was a small flop), and that I am putting him on either A-K or A-Q, too. But once I bet the flop and he raised it, I knew where he was with the hand.

Why did he make such a huge raise? If he put me on a big overpair, he may have figured that I would play it, but I didn't. He also knew that if he flat called, I would shut down if I didn't hit anything, so he may as well try to get me to play the hand on the flop. Also, you never want to give a free card in a tournament.

Jay knew that he had the pot won on the flop, so why not take it right then? Why give me a chance to bust him if one of my cards came off on the turn? ♠

PRACTICE HAND 11

You are Player B. You are holding two kings in the middle stage of a $1,000 tournament. You raised before the flop and Player A called.

The flop comes:

SCENARIO ONE

Player A checks. What do you do? A lot of players will check the ace on the flop. You also check.

SCENARIO TWO

This time you are Player A in first position with the kings. What do you do? You check because the ace is on the board. Player B probably also checks; a good player will check his ace on the flop if the raiser has checked in front of him. Now, suppose the turn comes with the 2♣. In a tournament, you check again. Player B probably will bet it, although he may not bet until fifth street. He knows that you don't have an ace and he may try to trap you on the end. But if an ace comes on the flop, you are through with the hand and will only play it for a showdown. ♠

PRACTICE HAND 12

In the middle stage of a no-limit tournament, you are dealt two kings for the third time. You raised before the flop. This time, you are determined to win with them.

Your hand:

The flop comes:

SCENARIO ONE

This time, you lead with the kings in the hope that an opponent holds a hand such as A♠ Q♦ or K♥ Q♥, hands that a player might call a raise with. If one of those hands is out, then you might get a play when you bet. Suppose that the 6♥ comes on the turn.

Now, you want to make a good-sized bet because you don't want to give anybody a chance to make two pair.

SCENARIO TWO

Suppose you're up against a player who stood your pre-flop raise with pocket queens. Some tournament players think that queens are the holy nuts and will even reraise with them. But since nobody reraised before the flop, you go with the kings and then try to shut them out on fourth street with a big bet.

There is also the chance that someone holds a K-J suited and will call your opening bet on a straight draw. Although he will probably call you on the flop, if you put in a big bet at fourth street, he will throw away the hand—unless he is a horrible player, that is. In no-limit or pot-limit hold'em, you can freeze out the draws on the turn, whereas in limit hold'em you cannot do that. ♠

PRACTICE HAND 13

This hand came up at the World Series when Hans "Tuna" Lund and I were involved in a hand. Tuna raised the pot from early position and it was passed all the way to me on the button.

I flat called him with:

The flop came:

THE SCENARIO

Tuna led at the pot with the:

What would you do? I flat called the bet. On the turn, he led at the pot again. This time, I moved over the top of him and he folded his hand.

ANALYSIS

It isn't wrong to take a chance once in a while. You hear so many people say, "Every time I have kings, an ace comes on the flop." If an ace comes, so what? Just throw away the hand. In this example, I played to win a big pot, and was able to extricate $2,700 from my opponent.

I knew that Tuna was likely to be holding A-Q or A-K before the flop, but there was a pretty good chance that I held the best hand, even though kings is the second-best pair you can be dealt.

In limit, pot-limit, and no-limit hold'em tournaments, it is not unusual for players to raise from early position with an A-Q. I don't suggest raising with it in a full ring, but five-handed or less, I will raise with the hand.

At a full table, I think that hands such as A-Q, A-J, or A-10 (suited or unsuited) in the first four seats are like 2-3. Why? Because if you stand a raise with them, where are you? It seems that when you start with the worst hand, you invariably flop a pair to it and then you're stuck in the pot. You try to avoid that situation by not playing these types of hands in early position, especially in a no-limit hold'em tournament. ♠

PRACTICE HAND 14

You are sitting in early position, the first three or four seats, in the early stage of a no-limit tournament. How do you proceed with this hand:

Do you bring it in with a raise, or do you just limp in?

SCENARIO ONE

My suggestion is that you limp with a pair of jacks (or tens) in this situation. If you raise and get reraised, what are you going to do with the hand? If you don't get raised, you could flop a jack and win a big pot, because nobody will put you on that big a hand to start with. You take the chance, of course, of having a player coming in with something like a little ace or K-Q and beating you. If someone outflops you and beats you, you would have been beaten anyway, but by not raising before the flop, you will lose less money if you are outflopped.

Of course, if you had raised before the flop, they may not have played those little-ace or K-Q hands, but your bigger worry is getting reraised and being forced to throw away the hand when you have money invested in the pot.

SCENARIO TWO

Now, suppose that you are sitting in fifth position and it has been passed to you. In that case, I would raise with the jacks whether or not it is early in the tournament. There is a big difference between these two situations: In this scenario, you already have four people out of the pot and there are only four players sitting behind you.

Early in the tournament when the antes are $25-$50, you might raise $150-to-$200 with the jacks. You have $10,000 in front of you, so that amount would be a reasonable raise. You don't make huge raises of $4,000, for example, early in a tournament. You make the small raise because you think that you have the best hand before the flop.

You are trying to do one of two things: either win the pot right there; or get called and win the pot as it develops. After all, the jacks aren't the best hand that you can have, and you couldn't even call with them on a lot of flops.

SCENARIO THREE

You are in the late stages of a tournament with the two jacks in your hand. How do you play them? Later in the tournament, you definitely want to raise with the two jacks. Say that you are playing at a shorthanded table with six or fewer players. Four tables are left in the tournament and each one of them is shorthanded.

In this case, you have to play the jacks much stronger than you would have played them earlier, although you don't necessarily want to commit your whole stack with the jacks.

PRACTICE HAND 15

At last, you have made it to the final table in a no-limit hold'em tournament. The table is six-handed, and you look down at this hand on the button:

The action is passed to you. What do you do?

ANALYSIS

A very famous tournament player that I know has a favorite move at the final table of a tournament—and there are a lot of players who use this same move. When they are around back and have a pair of fives or sixes, for example, they invariably move in their whole stacks when it is passed to them. I think that this is the most horrible play that I have ever seen in hold'em.

When you have worked that hard to get to the final table, why take the chance of losing your whole stack with a small pair? If the first four of five players in front of you don't have anything, there's a decent chance that one of the players behind you *will* have something. I have seen it happen time and time again: A player loses his entire stack because he moves in with all of his chips.

In this situation, it might be okay to make a baby raise, or even a decent-sized raise. For example, say that the antes are $200 and the blinds are $400-$800 at a six-handed table. There is $2,400 in the pot. You have $15,000 in front of you. If you want to raise, why not bring it in for $3,000? That's plenty — if you get reraised, you can get away from the hand; if you get outflopped, you can get away from it. But what are you going to do if you move in your whole stack and get called?

People are always talking about the fact that A-K is only an 11-to-10 underdog to a pair. But what they don't realize is that if you have two sixes, for example, and your opponent has a 7-8, the 7-8 also is only an 11-to-10 dog to your pair of sixes. It isn't just the A-K that is the underdog: *Any* two overcards are only an 11-to-10 under-dog to a pair. And if the overcards are suited, they are a slightly smaller dog to the pair. These numbers are what make moving in your whole stack with a pair such as sixes such a horrible play.

AN EXAMPLE FROM THE WORLD SERIES

At the final table of the 1993 World Series of Poker, John Bonetti, Jim Bechtel, and Glenn Cozen were playing three-handed at the final table. Bonetti raised before the flop with A-K and Cozen folded. Playing three-handed, Bechtel did what he was supposed to do: He called with pocket sixes. The flop came with a six and a king in it. Bonetti bet and Bechtel flat called him.

If you know your players, the flat-call in this situa-tion is the single biggest signal in the world. Jim Bechtel is a great player, and I know that he plays all of his big hands from behind. He lets you get yourself involved be-fore he does anything. His hands are weaker when he is leading than when he is check-calling. The worst hand that he could have had in this situation was a tie-hand, an A-K.

Phil Hellmuth and I were watching the action on the

TV monitor when this hand came up, and when Bonetti bet and Bechtel just called, I said to Phil, "Bonetti had better shut down right now." But he didn't. He moved in his whole stack on the turn. Bechtel won the hand, of course, and Bonetti came in third to Cozen. ♠

PRACTICE HAND 16

Suppose you are in middle position during the second level of a $500 buy-in tournament. Nobody has entered the pot. You look down at the following:

You haven't caught a hand in quite a while, so you decide to raise to try to pick up the pot. An opponent reraises behind you. What do you do?

You fold.

Why? Because you cannot stand a reraise before the flop with an A-Q in the opening rounds. Early in the tournament when I'm in middle to late position, if there are other limpers in the pot, I'll consider taking a cheap flop with the hand, but I won't raise with it. If there are no limpers, I like to bring it for a modest raise of about three times the size of the big blind. If anyone comes over the top of me, I fold.

If you catch either an ace or a queen on the flop, you will be in a bind as to what to do if someone bets at you. Why put yourself in that situation? You want to avoid having to make tricky decisions. Suppose you have flopped a queen and an early position raiser makes a big bet at the pot. Ask yourself what he could have, particularly if he's willing to jeopardize a lot of chips. People usually are not willing to risk getting broke early in a tournament unless they have a big pocket pair.

If I flop top pair and am the first to act, I usually will

make a pot-sized bet on the flop, but if I get played with, I usually will shut down. In fact it's easier to play *any* pair from up front than A-Q because a small to medium pair plays so easily after the flop—no set, no bet—whereas an A-Q or A-J require a lot of judgement if you get any action on the flop.

Later in the tournament, particularly when you're playing at a shorthanded table, A-Q goes up in value. When you're either short-stacked or are up against a short stack, you might have to take a stand with the hand.

ANALYSIS

Ace-queen is a trouble hand that should be played with caution. During the first levels of play in a nine or ten-handed game you don't want to put a lot of money in the pot with an A-Q (suited or unsuited) from an early position. Treat being suited as a bonus, something that should not change how you play the hand. Although I prefer suited cards when I play an A-Q, A-J or A-10, I value their ranks more than their suitedness. ♠

PRACTICE HAND 17

You are playing in a $2,000 tournament and are dealt:

SCENARIO ONE

The action is passed to you on the button. What do you do? I treat K-Q like 2-3, like it's the plague in no-limit hold'em, unless everybody passes to me on the button. Then, I might raise the two blinds with the hand, but that is the only place that I would raise with it. Although K-Q suited is better than K-Q offsuit, being suited still doesn't change the type of hand that it is.

SCENARIO TWO

You are on the button with K-Q. A player raises in front of you. What do you do? I surely would not stand a raise with this hand or raise with it myself. Here is the trap that you get into: Suppose you raise with the hand and someone calls you.

The flop comes:

Now, what are you going to do? You have top pair with second kicker. You don't have anything! There is a good chance that, since you were called before the flop, you are beaten already by someone who has the A-Q.

ANALYSIS

In no-limit hold'em, K-Q is a trap hand. Unless you flop J-10-9, A-J-10, two kings and a queen, or even two pair, you're in dire straits with this hand. The K-Q is a hand that you never want to play in a full ring game, in particular. The Q-J is the same type of hand. In fact, I give a little more value to the J-10 because you can make more straights with the hand than you can make with the K-Q or Q-J.

I wouldn't stand a raise with J-10, but I might play it in late position.

SCENARIO THREE

You are in the little blind with the K-Q. Everybody else has passed. What do you do?

In this case, you can raise the big blind, even though you are out of position and will have to act first after the flop. Some players will call a small raise from the big blind with hands that aren't very good because they already have money in the pot, but the chances are good that you'll win the pot right there with your pre-flop raise.

PRACTICE HAND 18

You're dealt these pocket cards:

In order to play an ace with a wheel card profitably, the right set of circumstances should be in place. Ace-little suited (or unsuited) is not a hand that you should play from an early position. It is of little value to you from up front because if an ace comes on the flop and you bet it and get played with, you have no kicker.

Obviously the best flop for ace-small suited is three to your suit or three wheel cards. But the odds are so great against getting that ideal flop that if you play ace-small every time you get it, you will be a big loser to the hand.

SCENARIO ONE

Suppose you are in middle to late position and a couple of limpers are in the pot. Since it is developing into a multiway pot, you might limp with ace-small and see the flop cheaply. If you get a good flop to it in multiway action, you have the chance to win a nice pot. You don't want to stand a raise with A-4 and you don't want to play it heads up. Therefore when you call a limp bet, be prepared to throw your hand away if someone raises.

Folding against a raise should be a part of your thinking even before you limp into the pot.

SCENARIO TWO

Suppose you're in the cutoff seat or on the button and no one has entered the pot. Should you raise with ace-small? No. You don't want to put yourself in a situation where you cannot get rid of this type of hand before the flop. Personally, I never play this hand strongly. (In no-limit circles we call it a sucker hand.)

Let's say that you raised on the button with it and the small blind calls the raise. What could he have? He probably has an ace in his hand or a pocket pair. And almost any kicker that he has with his ace will be higher than your wheel card. If his kicker also is a wheel card, you still are not a favorite to the hand most of the time if an ace falls.

ACE-SMALL IN LATE POSITION

Can you ever play ace-small from the last two positions? Yes, if no one else has entered the pot. But you don't raise with it, you limp. As I have maintained for years, if the four or five players in front of you don't have a hand, there's a good chance that one or two of the players behind you do have one. That is why you limp rather than raise with ace-small in late position—you cannot stand a reraise, you have to release it.

And if you raise and get called, you don't have a hand. If you want to go further with it, you have to be prepared to bluff with the hand unless you catch a flop to it. Why put yourself in that kind of situation?

Your goal is to always be in control.

ACE-SMALL IN THE BLIND

When you are in the small blind against the big blind only, you have three options: raise, fold or call. If you just call, you might get yourself into trouble. If you fold, you stay out of trouble. If you raise, you might win the pot right there. It depends on how you feel about it. If you have observed that your opponent usually defends his blind, forget about raising.

Consider limping against this type of opponent. If he is someone who raises all the time, he might raise just because you limped. Sometimes, depending on the type of player he is, you can reraise him.

Other times, against a different player, fold if he raises. What you decide to do depends on the kind of read you put on your opponent.

ACE-MIDDLE CARD

What about playing hands like A-6, A-7, or A-8? None of these ace-middle-card hands can make a straight. Your best result is the nut flush if the hand is suited, or two pair if you hit your kicker.

You're just throwing your money away if you play them.

PRACTICE HAND 19

AN ACE-SMALL CARD SCENARIO IN A MAJOR NO-LIMIT HOLD'EM TOURNAMENT

At the 2002 Hall of Fame tournament in heads-up no-limit action, Howard Lederer held A♦ 4♦. Peter Costa had K-6 offsuit.

The flop came:

Costa bet $30,000 and Lederer raised all-in.

"I can't find a reason to lay the hand down," Costa said and called the raise. The turn and river brought Lederer no help with either a diamond or an ace and Costa won the title.

PRACTICE HAND 20

ANOTHER ACE-SMALL CARD SCENARIO IN A BIG NO-LIMIT HOLD'EM TOURNAMENT

At the Four Queens Classic in 1996, Doyle Brunson and I were playing heads-up for the title in the $5,000 no-limit hold'em event.

I looked down at:

I raised a significant amount before the flop. Doyle called with:

The flop came:

Doyle was the first to act and he bet into me with his two pair. I flopped the top pair *and* the nut flush draw. I moved all in on him. Doyle called.

On the river the board looked like this:

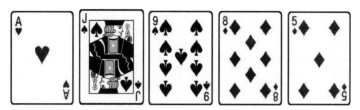

When the 8♦ came on the turn and the 5♦ came on the river, my big pair with a big draw bit the dust. Doyle's two pair stood up to win the pot and the championship.

This hand just proves once again that the luck factor comes into play in all of poker. You might make the right play with the best hand, but that doesn't guarantee that you're going to get the right results.

Just ask me. ♠

8

TALES FROM T. J.

When you've been on the road for as many years as T. J. Cloutier, you're bound to pick up a lot of stories along the way. Tales about the road gamblers, the tournament players, the big guys and the little guys, their bad beats and their big wins. Dramas with a cast of characters composed of villains and heroes playing out their hands against the colorful backdrops of smoky backrooms and elegant casinos. Some of them faded the white line from Dallas to Houston while others made their marks on the big-time tournament circuit, each taking his cues from Lady Luck in the topsy-turvy world of poker.

On the next few pages, you'll read some of the good ol' boy stories that T. J. is famous for—the tales that he tells his many friends across the tables of poker rooms around the world.

JACK "TREE TOP" STRAUS AND HIS PRINCIPLE

Little Red Ashey and I were staying at the Anthony Motel in Hot Springs, Arkansas, while we were going to the horse races. "Let's go next door," says Little Red. "Jack Straus is there." So we went to the room next to us and had just started talking with Jack when we heard a pounding on the door. Jack opened the door and let a guy in.

You had to know Jack to understand this story. He borrowed and loaned a lot of money in his time, and it was always on what we called "principle." Principle meant that Jack set up a certain day to pay back his loan, and he only paid it on that exact day. Seems that Jack had borrowed $5,000 from this fellow and the guy had come over to dun him for the money. "I've still got thirty days to pay that off," Jack said, "so quit dunning me." And the guy left. As the first man was going down the stairs, a second man was coming up them. The door was still open so Jack let him in.

"I'm down on my luck," the man tells Jack. "Could you loan me $10,000?" And Jack peeled the $10,000 right out of his pocket and gave it to him! I couldn't explain Jack Straus any better than telling this story: This is the way that he thought. One time when we were on the golf course, he told me that he liked me because I was like him. "I'm broke one day and have a fortune the next day," he said, "and I don't give a damn." ♠

GEORGE MCGANN, ROBBER-PLAYER

George loved to play poker, but he was a stone killer. He stood about five foot eight or nine and weighed about 145 pounds, and he always wore a suit and tie. And he always carried two guns with him. One day George was playing at the AmVets in Dallas and he got broke. So he pulled out his gun and robbed everybody at the game, took every dime they had.

"Boys, I'm short," he says as he took their money. But the kicker to this story is that the very next day, he came back into the game, sat down and played with these same guys—and nobody said a word!

Some years later when George was in his forties, he and his wife were murdered at the same time. The rumor was that he had been collecting money for somebody and somehow they had set him up.

Around Texas, they said that George had been accused of killing about thirty or forty people, but he was never actually convicted of murder. ♠

TROY INMAN, THE "PROTECTOR"

The first time I went to Dallas to play poker, I played at the AmVets. A very notorious guy named Troy Inman was running the game. I was playing with the great players in those days, guys like Bob Hooks, Kenny Smith, Dicky Carson, Bill Bonds, and Bill Smith.

It was a helluva game. I happened to win $8,000 the first time I played in that no-limit hold'em game, but when it came time for me to leave, I had to walk down three flights of stairs to get out of the place. And it was in a pretty bad area down in the lower Greenville section of Dallas near Highway 30.

As I was leaving, I got to wondering if I was gonna get out of the joint with all that money—Troy was pretty notorious for hiding around corners and shooting people and stuff like that.

Then Troy says, "Wait a minute, T. J. With you packing that much cash on you, maybe I'd better walk down with you and be sure you get in your car." So, he pulls out his pistol in case somebody came after us. As we were walking down the stairs, I was more afraid of the guy protecting me than I was of having somebody from the outside rob me! But I got away with the money okay.

I'll tell you another story about Troy Inman. He was in and out of money. One time he left Dallas going to Shreveport and stopped off in Tyler, Texas, where he saw Henry Bowen, who had bought a house there. After he left Bowen's house, Troy went to a joint down on the river in Shreveport where they had all the girls doing the dancing, but they weren't nude, they wore tops.

Anyway, he tipped off $1,000 in one night to these girls. They would come and sit with him at his table, and he'd give them $20 here, $20 there, and he'd give the head girl $40. But the kicker to the story is that he was broke at the time. He had stopped off in Tyler to borrow the $1,000 from Bowen! ♠

A VERY UNLUCKY
DAY IN ODESSA

A lot of people in Dallas were afraid of Troy. He had a sneaky reputation; you never knew what to expect from him. So, there was this card game one time in either Midland or Odessa, the site doesn't really matter. Nobody could play in this game except these rather notorious men from the area, the drug dealers and the bookmakers. And they were all what we called "packing" in Texas— they were all armed.

Seems that one guy accused another one of cheating, which they were all doing, and the guns started blazing. Two guys were killed right there in the game, and another guy was shot going out the front door. All the houses were right next to each other, so the people next door heard all the gun shots and called for the cops. The man that was shot going out of the place started pounding on their door to ask for help, standing there just bleeding to death. The guy opened up the door and killed him with a shotgun, thinking that he was trying to break in.

That's one gambler who had a very unlucky day. Next time you think you're having a bad day in poker, just think about this guy! ♠

CRAWFISH AND POKER IN BATON ROUGE

I was playing down in Baton Rouge years ago, where everything closes at 2:00 a.m. Across the bridge there was an all-night dance hall and restaurant that served great boiled crawfish on big tin platters. Right next to the dance hall, I noticed a door with a peep hole in it. I looked through it and saw a poker game going on, so I knocked on the door. "Looks like a helluva game you're playin' in there," I said to the bouncer. "I've just got one question to ask you—if I happen to get lucky and win the money, can I get out of here with it?"

"In the five years I've been doing this job," he said, "you're the first one who's ever asked me that question. I would suggest that you don't play." So, I left. But most of the games that we played in around Texas were pretty secure and we never had any problems.

We played at Charlie Bissell's for 11 years and the police only raided us one time. It was a clean environment. He put on a brand new table top every two weeks, and he had the best food you've ever eaten in a poker game. Bissell ran a $5-$10-$25-blind poker game and at least once a week, we had $100,000 on the table. He would start out with a $5,000 buy-in, and if he lost one quarter in the game, he would add another $5,000 to his stack, so there was always plenty of money to shoot at.

For $5, you could cut the cards. The way it worked was that if you put $5 in the pot, you had the right to cut the deck before the next card was dealt. You could do this at any point in the game. Every time that Charlie was on the draw, he always cut the cards, so you always knew where you stood with him. ♠

THE POKER PLAYER WITH A SENSE OF HUMOR

Everett Goulsby was a famous man in Texas, and the way he acted in a poker game made him the funniest man I've ever seen in a game. He loved to brag so much that whenever he won a hand, he'd tell everybody around the table about it. We were playing down in Tyler one time and all the top players were there— Little Red Ashey, Bob Hooks, Cowboy Wolford, Johnny Wheeler. All the well-known players in Texas were playing, and Everett was winning pots.

George Lambert was running the game. He had a big gallon jug of booze sitting on the side of the table and he would take a sip or two before each hand. George was sitting on Everett's left and Johnny Wheeler sat to his right. Every time Everett won a pot, he would turn to Johnny and brag to him about how he had won that hand. And then George would reach over and take a $100 chip off of Everett's stack and put it in with his own. This happened every single time Everett won a hand.

But the funniest part of the story is that everybody in the game except Everett saw it happen—and nobody ever told him!

Everett was a beaut. He made sure that he made an "appearance" every time we played poker. He'd wait to show up until about thirty minutes after the game started. He might have played with everybody in the game the day before, but he'd walk around the table and pat everybody on the back and say hello.

But as soon as you beat him one time, he'd say, "You dirty so-and-so, you'll be broke and sleeping in the street and I'll still have money."

Everett was one of the best head-up players that ever played poker. The last time I saw him was just after he got out of jail from the 22 months that he did for book-making. "I'm just an old man now. I don't do anything anymore," he said to me. Part of his probation was that he couldn't go to Dallas County.

The last that any of us heard about him, he had left the country because the cops were after him on other charges. ♠

HEAD-UP AGAINST THE BEST

When you talk about the old timers who were great head-up players, the names Everett Goulsby and Jack Straus always come up. We used to say, "If Everett's lips are moving, he's lying." I went to him one time and asked, "How many times have you played Straus head-up?"

"I've played him three times and I beat him every time," he said. About a month later, I asked Jack the same question.

"I broke Everett all three times," he answered. So then, I had to figure out which one was telling the truth. Personally, I believed Straus.

Speaking of head-up play, I was at the World Series one year when Bobby Hoff was playing Betty Carey in a head-up match. This happened back when Dorfman, the multimillionaire from New York, was backing Betty. They were playing in the Sombrero Room at Binion's Horseshoe and they had at least $50,000 each on the table. On the first day they played, I saw Betty make a couple of draws on Bobby and vice versa. Bobby thought that he was going to get to play her again the next day, but Amarillo Slim cut in on him and played Betty and shut Bobby out of the game.

I think Bobby Hoff is one of the greatest head-up players in the world. The last time I saw him play real big, before he started playing in Las Vegas, was at the Commerce Club in Southern California. He played with all the best. ♠

LITTLE RED AND FIVE-CARD STUD

Until just a few years ago, I thought that Little Red Ashey was the best card player I'd ever seen play—period, bar none— because of his judgment. He was about 6'5" tall and weighed almost three hundred pounds, had a deep voice and flaming red hair. One day, Little Red went to Tyler to play in Lambert's game and I took a piece of him. Before the game started, he told me, "T. J., I'm gonna show you how to play tight today." And he did. If he had A-K in the first five seats, he wouldn't put the first quarter in. Yet, he won $3,800 in the game.

At one time, Little Red was rated as the best stud player in the United States. Five-card stud, not seven-card stud, was the game they played back then. A lot of people talk about Sarge Ferris being a great stud player. He and Little Red used to play in the same game with all the old timers in Shreveport, guys like Red Wynn, McCorquodale, Slim Etheridge, Homer Marcotte, all the top five-card stud players that were there. And Little Red was beating them all.

Then when he started coming to Vegas to play, Sarge would put up a bankroll for him. "If anybody wants to play five-card stud," Sarge told him, "you go and play them. There's always money in the cage for you." But they only got it on a couple of times. George Huber tried it one time, and he didn't like it—he was supposed to be a good stud player, but he couldn't play Little Red.

Ashey also played hold'em as well as any man I've seen play the game. He had that rare judgment. He could lay down three of a kind one time, and then call you with a pair of fours the next time, and be right on both sides of the issue. Little Red is still around, but he doesn't play cards very much any more. ♠

WHERE A LOT OF STORIES BEGIN AND END

They used to say in Dallas that a lot of stories begin and end with Everett Goulsby. Everett had what we call a real "sizz" factor. If he got stuck in a game, he was liable to play every hand for the next three hours. George Huber was staying with Everett at his house one time, so he drove George over to play in the game. Everett didn't want to play himself, but he took one-half of George's play.

Well, George got in the game for $2,000 and lost it all. Everett was sitting in the front room in his slippers and he says, "George, I'll show you how to play this game." George told Everett okay, but that he wanted twenty-five percent of him.

So Everett gets in the game and before long, he's in $26,000 with $8,000 left. I'm sitting in the game and we're down to five-handed with Everett sitting on my left. I had about $8,000 left, too. It was passed to me on the button and I look down at J-9 of clubs. So I made it $700 to go. Everett's playing every hand and he just saddled right in for the $700. The flop came 10-8-7 of clubs! Everett moved in and I never had to make a bet. He had called with 10-7 offsuit and made two pair against my straight flush. And that was the end of Everett Goulsby for that day.

Then just before they were leaving to go home, Everett goes over to George Huber and says, "Okay, George, you owe me twenty-five percent of $26,000."

"I'm only in for the first $1,000," George says. "And twenty-five percent of $1,000 is $250." Everett went home, threw George's suitcase on the lawn, and that was the end of their relationship.

After I finished second in the Big One at the World Series in 1985, George called me in Dallas wanting to know if I'd loan him $2,000 to play the game in Houston. So I got the guys on the phone who were running the game and told them to give him the $2,000, that I'd be there in a few days to bring them the money. Later, I heard that George played two hands, cashed out his chips, and left with my money. And I haven't heard from him since.

♠

KENNY "WHATTA PLAYER" SMITH

Kenny was a big chess player in Texas and he just loved to play poker, played poker for years. He always wore a silk top hat that was supposed to have been from the theater where Abraham Lincoln was assassinated. He even had certification on it. Kenny would wear that hat in all the big tournaments, and every time he won a pot he would stand up from the table and yell, "What a player!" And that's how he got his nickname.

We were playing in a hand at the AmVets one time when Bob Hooks limped in and Ken Smith raised the pot up a pretty good amount of money. It came back to Hooks and he moved in his whole stack with two kings.

Ken put the stall on Hooks for about three minutes, didn't look like he was ever going to act on his hand. So Hooks looks over and grabs Ken's cards out of his hand and sees two aces—and he moved Ken's chips into the pot himself! So Ken never had to put his own money in, Hooks put it in for him. I'll bet that was the only time that Hooks ever lost a hand when he put the money in for both players. ♠

THE MYSTERY HAND PLAY

Bob Hooks, a great player who came in second one year at the World Series, and I were playing in Shreveport one time when a play that I call my "mystery hand" came up. Wayne Edmunds was in the game with us and we were playing pot-limit hold'em. We'd been playing for quite a few hours and there was a lot of money on the table when a hand came up where I had the stone nuts on fourth street.

I had $5,000 in front of me and made a $2,000 bet. Wayne had a habit of putting his head down after he called a bet, so he never saw what was going on anywhere else at the table. As I was making my bet, the dealer grabbed my cards and threw them in the muck! Of course, Wayne didn't see it happen. "What do I do now?" I was wondering.

The dealer burned and then turned the next card. I have big hands and I just kept them out in front of me like I was protecting my cards. I bet my last $3,000 and Wayne threw his hand away. I won the pot without any cards!

Bob and everybody else at the table except Wayne had seen what happened, but nobody said a thing. And that's the story behind my mystery-hand play. ♠

THE WORST BAD BEAT OF ALL TIME

One year at the Bicycle Club, I was playing in a no-limit hold'em side game with Al Krux, a very fine player who has made several appearances at the final table at the World Series. But Al wasn't doing very well in this game, and he was losing most of his money. He brought in the hand for his final money, $435. Two seats away there was a player who was holding his hand up in the air so that he could see it while a masseuse was giving him a rub down, and his opponent to his left could see it, too. This player decided not to call and threw his hand away.

It got around to me sitting just to the left of the dealer on the button, and I called the $435 with two tens. "This might be the best hand here, since Al's all in and I can't lose any more than $435," I thought. But the dealer didn't see that I had called and so she dropped the deck on the muck. She asked for a ruling and the floorman said that she had to reshuffle all of the cards except the two hands that Al and I were holding. The flop came K-10-4. Al had pocket kings and I had pocket tens. On fourth street came another ten, giving me four tens and winning the money. But the kicker to this story is that the guy who had held his hand up before the flop had been dealt the two tens that came out on the flop after the reshuffle!

The only way that I could possibly have a win against Al's hand was for the dealer to make a mistake, reshuffle those two tens back into the deck, and bring them back out again on the flop and fourth street. That ended Al's day—and I never won another pot that session. If you can think of a worse bad beat story than this one, I'd like to hear it! ♠

SPEAKING OF BAD BEATS ...

Back in Texas there was a very famous poker player named Doc Ramsey, who couldn't stand to take a bad beat. He was the type of guy who would run around the room telling everybody what a bad beat he had taken and how he took it. If he saw you across the street walking the other way from him, he would cross the street just to tell you his bad-beat story.

One night he took a pretty bad beat and tried to tell everybody in the room about it, but nobody would listen to him.

"Doc," we said, "We've heard it a million times and we don't want to hear it again."

So he got up from the table, went into the kitchen, and cornered the Chinese chef. We all followed him and got a big kick out of watching him moaning to the chef, who didn't speak a word of English and just kept shaking his head as Doc rattled on. ♠

MR. BROOKS AND THE TWO JACKS

Years ago in Dallas, Charlie Hendricks, who was a known gambler around Texas at the time, came to play with us in our no-limit game. In the old days, Bob Brooks ran all of the gaming in Anchorage, Alaska, but he had been playing in our Dallas game for several years and we knew all of his moves.

He and Hendricks were playing in a five-way pot, and Mr. Brooks just flat called from the little blind. Now it was time for Charlie to act from the big blind. He looked down and found two jacks in the hole.

"I can win this pot right now," he said to himself. "They've all limped in, so I'll just put in a raise because I've got the best hand." So he raised about $400. Everybody passed, and then it got around to Mr. Brooks in the little blind. He moved all-in.

Now Charlie thinks to himself, "I've gotta have the best hand. Mr. Brooks would never have passed a big hand there in the little blind." But we all knew Mr. Brooks. He was sitting there with pocket aces. He had been playing a trap the whole time and didn't care about just winning $25 from each person. He broke Charlie on this pot. We were all laughing at the table, because it was the first time that Charlie had come to Dallas to play with us, and he didn't know how Mr. Brooks played. Nobody else on that table would have called with two jacks.

It was very hard to get any money out of Mr. Brooks at the poker table. We were playing in a side game once and I had two eights. I made a little token raise with them and Mr. Brooks and another player both called the raise.

The flop came 8-8-4. When you flop quads, it is customary to check-check-check in the hope that somebody will catch up with you so that you can win a little something with the hand. But I decided to lead with the hand and bet $200 on the flop. Mr. Brooks called.

Fourth street brought a deuce. I bet $1,000 and he called that, too. On the end came a 10. I bet $2,500 and Mr. Brooks moved in on me. He had pocket tens and had filled on the river.

Because I had led at the pot with a huge hand, I made about $10,000 on the hand. If I had checked it all the way to the river, Mr. Brooks would have made a little bet on the end and I would have raised him. Then he would either have called me or made a small raise because there wouldn't have been enough money in the pot for him to put any real money in on the end. The way the hand worked out was just perfect for me. ♠

THE BEST WOMAN PLAYER IN THE WORLD

There has never been a female player that could touch Betty Carey. She was the best woman player that I have ever seen at no-limit hold'em. There are a lot of very good female limit hold'em and seven-card stud players, but Betty was in a class by herself at no-limit. She took on all of the top players and played them head-up. Like Barbara Enright, she had a lot of guts.

Betty also had the biggest win anybody ever made at Bissell's—$51,000 in a $5-$10-$25 no-limit hold'em game one night. She had all the hands in the right spots and the guys weren't giving her credit for being the player that she was. She ate them alive. I was happy to get out of there even.

Betty was a consummate gambler. She gambled high, high, high. One night, she came into the Stardust when Dody Roach and I were at the craps table. When she saw us, she sat down her bags, and blew $60,000 before she even checked into the hotel. Dody was betting more than I was, and she was betting more than Dody.

Yes, Betty was a gambler. ♠

THE WORST DECISION IN THE HISTORY OF POKER

I was in tournament stress mode at a big tournament one year when something happened to me that shouldn't happen to a dog. I had never played the tournament before, but John Bonetti asked me to come out for it, so I was there for the last three days.

More than 400 players were in a limit-hold'em event, and we were down to six-handed play at the $2,000-$4,000 limits. I raised it up to $4,000 before the flop and it got around to the button. The guy on the button didn't see the raise and put in $2,000. The dealer reminded him that it was $4,000 to go since I had raised.

The button said, "Well, my hand isn't good enough for that," and grabbed back his $2,000. Then he threw his cards face down and they went into the muck, so that all you could see was the ends of his cards.

The floorman was standing there and said to the dealer, "Don't kill that hand." So the dealer pulled the cards out of the muck and the floorman instructed the button to either leave the $2,000 in the pot and muck his hand, or put in the rest of the $4,000 and play out the hand. The button decided that rather than losing the $2,000, he would call with his K-J.

The flop came A-Q-10. He flopped the straight. I had A-K so, of course, I would have played the hand anyway six-handed. When the hand started, I had $12,000, and when it was over I had $2,000. Essentially, it cost me any chance of winning the event.

I didn't put up a fuss at the time, because I usually don't do that kind of thing. But when it was all over and I had been knocked out, I asked the floorman how he could have made a decision that allowed a player to pull cards out of the muck that were face down.

The tournament director excused the decision with, "Well, this is not the Horseshoe. We do things differently here."

Then I really got hot.

"Do you know how many times this has happened in a tournament with over 400 players, when people have put money in the pot and then pulled it back? Are you going to tell me that you made that decision every time?"

No, he couldn't see them every time.

"Then how could you have made that decision at a time when the big money is at stake?" I asked.

The only decision that could have been made was that the hand was dead when it touched the muck. Letting that hand live is the worst decision I've ever seen in a tournament. ♠

THE TOUGHEST TABLE IN TOURNAMENT POKER

In the $5,000 tournament at the last Stairway to the Stars tournament that was held, the action got down to two tables, 18 people. My starting table was perhaps the toughest table in the history of poker. There were Doyle Brunson, Chip Reese, Stu Ungar, Jack Keller, Berry Johnston, Dewey Tomko, David Baxter, Hamid Dastmalchi, and me. Among the nine of us, there were more than 150 tournament victories. The caliber of players was such that, if any one of us had made just the slightest error, he would have been gone.

The other table was full of unknowns, nobodies on the tournament circuit. When it got down to the final three, Hamid had the lead with $50,000 and Berry and I had about $25,000 each. Luckily, I won it. I seem to do better at tough tables because they tend to keep me in line.

Another tough tournament line-up happened at the Queens Classic $5,000 buy-in final event in 1996. The final four were Doyle Brunson, Chip Reese, Eric Seidel, and me. This time, Doyle won it and I came in second. In the final hand, I held the A♠ 2♠ and he had a J-9 offsuit. The flop came A-J-9 with two spades, and we got it all in. Doyle's J-9 held up. As far as skill goes, this was the toughest final four I've ever come across. ♠

9

A CONVERSATION WITH T.J. CLOUTIER

BY DANA SMITH

If you ask players on the tournament circuit who they think are the best poker players in the world, T.J. Cloutier's name always comes up. Not because he's won the Big One— he hasn't, although he's come mighty close to winning it several times. And not because he's made the most money at the World Series—he hasn't, although he was the first player to make more than $1 million at it without winning the main event. T.J. Cloutier's name is always mentioned because he is the player that they all respect and fear.

His skills have been honed in the back rooms of Texas, in games where they were all carrying guns. His card sense has been sharpened through years of beating the best of the road gamblers at no-limit hold'em. And his table demeanor has been polished on the rough surfaces of country roads as he faded the white line traveling to the next game.

T.J. is one of the last of the legendary road gamblers whose numbers are, unfortunately, dwindling each year.

He brings a wealth of experience, card skill, and natural ability to every game that he plays. But more importantly, he always brings along his knowledge of the thousands of players that he has faced head up in the twenty-one years that he has made his living as a professional poker player. And that sixth sense about what makes his opponents tick—that innate ability to put a player on a hand—is why his opponents fear him. It is as though he is looking at you through an invisible microscope, knowing what you are thinking, detecting your tells, delving into the the inner spaces of your mind. You know that he knows you, knows what you're going to do next. And he's going to use his encyclopedic memory of how you play to beat you.

I got to know T.J. first through hearsay, then by talking with him and Tom McEvoy while we were working on this book, and finally by observing him in action. All three encounters have been awesome. While T.J. and I were recording his life's story, I somehow had the feeling that I was sitting at the feet of a master, a master of people. And I knew that there was much that I could learn from the man whom Mansour Matloubi has called "the greatest living no-limit hold'em player in the world." Here is his story.

T.J. Cloutier graduated from Jefferson High School in Daly City, CA, where he was a three-letter man. At 6'3" tall, he was the center on the basketball team, played football, and still holds the home run record in baseball. So, were all the girls waiting in line for a date with him? "Well, when I was a senior, I dated Pat Kennedy, who later won the Miss California title," he modestly admits. "We had a study group of ten or fifteen kids that ran around together, and high school came very easy to me. It was when I got into college that I found out that you had to study."

T.J. entered the University of California at Berkeley on a baseball and football athletic scholarship, and played for Cal in the Rose Bowl in 1959 as a sophomore. But when his mother became ill, he dropped out of college to go to work and help his father pay some of her medical bills. Then the army snapped him up, since he no longer was a draft-deferred student.

T.J. gained his first experience playing poker when he was a caddy at the Lake Merced and San Francisco Country Clubs. When he and the other caddies came in from taking their loops (caddying), they played a form of poker in the caddy shack. One day, somebody passed around some "lucky bucks" from Artichoke Joe's, a cardroom in San Francisco. For $15, he received a $20 buy-in for the lowball game. So, at the age of 17 years, T.J. started playing poker in a public cardroom and by the time he was 19 years old, he was playing head-up draw poker against Artichoke Joe himself.

"When I began playing, all the games were no-limit, including no-limit lowball without the joker and no-limit high draw poker," he reflects. "Then when I entered college, I played poker at the Kappa Alpha house with Joe Capp, the Cal quarterback who later played in the NFL, and Bobby Gonzalez, who became a supervisor in San Francisco. I found out that I had a knack for the game, although I lost everything I had at the time. Actually, I was honing my skills at observation and getting to know people. I've always had a sort of photographic memory for how people play their hands in certain situations. If you and I had played poker together five years ago, I wouldn't remember your name, but I would remember your face and how you played your hands in different situations, your tendencies. It's a visual memory thing; I've always been very observant throughout my entire life."

So, you keep a book on players, I asked?

"No, it's nothing that formal. It's more like pages opening up in a book in my mind. And that helps, especially in no-limit games."

He then went on to play poker in the army, where he furthered his training at cards. When T.J. got out of the army, he walked into the office of the Montreal Allouettes and asked if he could try out with them. After checking out his record at Cal, the general manager told him, "We'll put you up for two weeks, and then you can come out and show us what you have." He went to one workout and made the team, after not having played any football for two years. The team paid his expenses until the training camp began, and he played first string tight end for the Allouettes until he was traded to the Toronto Argonauts.

Canadian football was a lot different from American football in those days. Thirteen Americans were suited up, along with 17 Canadians. "My value was that my father was born in Canada, so I could play as a Canadian— an American-trained Canadian was just what they were looking for."

The team had only 12 players going each way, leaving just six reserves, including the kickers and other special players. So, in addition to playing first string tight end, T.J. also was first backup to the defensive ends. "It's a rugged brand of football, wide open. When I was playing, you couldn't block for a pass receiver once he caught the ball past the line of scrimmage. The field was 110 yards long, the end zones were twenty yards deep, and the field was wider. You had to make a first down in the first two downs or else kick the ball, since there were only three downs. It was a real fast game, and everybody was in motion all the time."

Another different facet was that you couldn't block for a punt receiver; once he caught the ball, he was on his own. "You had to give the punt receiver five yards to catch the ball. So, the other team would circle him like the Indians circling the settlers, and as soon as he caught that ball, he was dead, flatter than a pancake."

T.J. played Canadian football for five years, until his knees gave out. Then he received a call from Victoria when they were trying to form the Continental Football League. Victoria offered him its coaching job, but he also would have to play. "Are you kidding?" he asked. "If I could still play, I'd be playing for Montreal or Toronto."

Of course, football wasn't the only game in town. A cardroom in Vancouver, B.C., spread a poker game called *sousem* a form of five-card stud. "In sousem, a four-card straight or a four-card flush beats one pair, so it puts a lot of action into the game," T.J. explained. "It was quite a game, no-limit. The only other game we played was no-limit ace-to-five lowball." And even that game wasn't the only one in town. "In Montreal, the Hebrew Businessmen's Club spread five-card stud. I was getting whipped pretty good, but it was all a part of the learning process," T.J. admits.

When he left Canada, T.J., his father, and his brother-in-law started Bets Quality Foods, an acronym for Bill,

Ed, and Tom (T. J.'s first name), and later brought T.J.'s brother in with them. "We used the money that I had left from football and my dad's retirement to start the business. Our slogan was 'Your Best Bet in Quality Foods.' We bought a huge freezer from Foster's, a big cafeteria chain in San Francisco, when they went out of business and rebuilt it in our warehouse to handle our frozen food. We had a big egg business, too, although you don't make much money from eggs. But when you're serving big hotels, you have to give them the eggs at a good price to keep their other business. I was working 16 hours a day— I would take orders, load trucks, and pick up and deliver products. Later, we merged with A & A Foods, and they stole us blind. My dad won an 11-count court case against them, but the owners left the country."

After suffering this bad beat, T.J. began delivering bread for Toscana and eventually wound up as night manager for Wonder Bread in San Francisco. "My first wife and I split up about that time, and I ended up heading for Texas with $100 in my pocket," he remembers. That was in 1976. "I went to work for six months as a derrick man on the oil rigs down there. On my off days, I was playing poker. Pretty soon, I was making more money at poker than I was on the rigs. I'd been freezing up there anyway, so that's how I moved into playing poker full time."

He played no-limit hold'em in Longview, Texas, and pot-limit hold'em in Shreveport, Louisiana, 51 miles away. T.J. had only played hold'em a few times before that. While he was playing lowball at the Cameo Club in Palo Alto, California, a club across the street tried three times to start a hold'em game, but the police came in and busted them every time.

Because of the good games in Shreveport, T.J. moved there to play poker every day at the Turf Club. "The games were much smaller than we're playing now. On Sundays, they would have a big game run by an old gambler named Harlan Dean who was well known in all the gambling places. He used to be George Barnes' partner in the bridge tournaments in Vegas, and he was one of the original hold'em players.

I ended up selling the chips, and if I got broke or something, he'd call up on a Sunday and ask, 'Well, we're broke, are we, ol' partner?' And I'd say, 'Well, Mr. Dean, I know you're not broke, but I am.' Then he'd say, 'Well, you come on by today and I'll give you some chips.' And if I got loser in the game, I could have the chip rack because he didn't want the game to end. That's when I started playing real serious poker."

In 1978, T.J. made his first trip to the World Series of Poker, although he didn't play in the championship tournament until 1983 (the year that Tom McEvoy won it). But the third year that he played for the World Championship (in 1985), he finished second to Bill Smith, with Berry Johnston taking third. "When it got down to three-handed, Berry Johnston had the best hand, an A-K. I had an A-J. The flop came K-J-little, and we got it all in. On the turn, I caught a jack and drew out on him to put him out of the tournament.

Then it got to two-handed and I had the lead against Bill. But the key hand of the whole match happened when I had two nines and he had two kings. He moved in and I called him with my nines. He won the pot and doubled up. Now he had a big lead, and I started chopping back at him. There were 140 players that year, so there was

$1,400,000 in chips; I got back to $350,000. Then Bill came in with a little raise, and I looked at an ace in my hand. I didn't even look at the other card, but made it look like I had. I just went over the top of him with the whole $350,000. I knew that he had to make a decision— if he made the wrong one, I'd be back even with him again. He had started drinking, and he gave away money when he was drinking. He called. When I looked back at my hand, my kicker was a three. And Bill had two threes. They held up and he won the title.

"He was one of the greatest players of all time, Bill Smith was. Bill was the tightest player you'd ever played in your life when he was sober. And when he was half-way drunk, he was the best player I'd ever played with. But when he got past that halfway mark, he was the worst player I'd ever played with. And you could always tell when he was past the halfway point because he started calling the flop. Say a flop came 7-4-10 — he would say, '21!' or some other remark like that. When he got up to take a walk, he would have a little hop in his step, a 'git up in his gittalong' we used to call it. And then you knew he was gone.

"But Bill had such great timing on his hands when he was younger and wasn't drunk, he was out of this world. He knew when to lay down three of a kind, when to call with a baby underpair with two or three overcards on the board. He was a fabulous player, but he became an alcoholic and that was that. You never worried about Bill when he was sober because you knew that he played A-B-C, tight, and you knew where he was all the time. The only time that you worried about him was when he was about halfway drunk, and then he'd play all the way to 'H'.

He'd make some fabulous plays, plays you couldn't believe. Bill Smith was a truly great player."

In those days, T.J. was living in Shreveport, playing poker every day. "In fact," he said, "I was having a gay old time. I was single then, and would go to the Louisiana Downs 100 out of the 105 days of the meet, and then go out and play poker every night. I learned more about poker in Shreveport than anywhere else in the world. There was a real good game on Sunday and a guy named Jim "Little Red" Ashey used to play in it. He's bigger than I am—about 6'5" tall and 300 pounds, but they called him Little Red because he started playing there when he was about 16 or 17 years old. I learned more from just watching him play than any other way." It was like sitting at the feet of the master, except that the master was not instructing T.J. "I was actually absorbing what Red did, and then suiting those moves to my own style, which was aggressive at times and passive at other times. You can't let them pigeon hole you, you know.

"A lot of people think that Sarge Ferris was the best five-card stud player in the world. Well, when Red was 17 years old, he was playing with Sarge, Corky McCorquodale, Homer Marcotte—all the big names in five-card stud used to play in Shreveport. And Little Red beat them all the time."

Marcotte was killed in Dallas. "Homer was called 'The Louisiana Man' because wherever he went, he would say, "I'm the Louisiana Man." He was shot dead by some guy about 5'5" tall in a Dallas bar back around 1978 over a $50 bar bill. The little guy kept dunning Marcotte for the $50 and Homer kept saying, 'Don't you know me? I'm the Louisiana Man. You don't dun me for $50.' Finally, this little guy had heard enough, went out to his car to get his gun, came back in, and shot Marcotte.

"Anyway, when Sarge went out to Vegas and won all that money, he put up a bankroll for Red while the World Series was on so that if Red came out, he'd have the money to play against anybody that wanted to play him. The only person I know of that they ever got a game on with was George Huber, and he didn't last two hours against Red. Lost about $40,000 to him. Of course, Red didn't come out very often because he hated to fly. You'd almost have to give him a shot like Mister T on the old A-Team show just to get him on an airplane. Red liked horses and sports betting, so all his money went there, and after he got into that, poker wasn't fast enough for him. But at one time, he was very well respected in poker, especially in the South."

A lot of good hold'em players came from the South, from the Sun Belt states. T.J. is one of the best of them. "While I was living in Shreveport, I found out about a real good game in Dallas that was run by a man that I will call The Big Texan. It was a $5-$10-$25 no-limit hold'em game with either a $500 or a $1,000 buy in. I used to drive the two hundred miles from Shreveport three days a week to play in that game." The first twelve times that he played in the game, he won. Then, on his next visit, the Big Texan told T.J., "I'm dropping the latch on you. If you don't give me half your play, you can't play here anymore." So, T.J. gave him half his action for his next ten visits—and he won all ten times.

"Then one day I went down there and out of the blue, the Big Texan said to me, 'I'm out today.' That rang a warning bell in my head. I knew that there was something going on, something was wrong. There were two new players in the game, so I just bought in for $500 in chips, played for about an hour, and hardly ever got into a pot. Then I left."

That was around the time that Bill Smith and T.J. became friends. Bill's wife, Cleta, was working at Mitsubishi Aircraft in New Orleans and introduced T.J. to Joy, whom he married in 1984. "That's the reason I moved to Dallas from Shreveport, not just because of the game but because Joy lived there. She was the personal secretary to the president of Mitsubishi."

Joy Cloutier has one daughter from a previous marriage, whom T.J. put through Texas A & M where she received her training as a petroleum engineer. Today, Joy travels with T.J. to most of the tournaments on the circuit. "Joy is amazing. I don't know what she does while I'm playing the tournaments, but the day does not have enough hours for her."

Lyle Berman was T.J.'s first tournament backer. At the time, Berman was backing Jack Keller and another player. When the second player fell out of their arrangement, Berman asked around to find out who else he might back. T. J's name was suggested, so he and Lyle spoke on the telephone and then met at the airport on the their way to the Bicycle Club's big tournament in 1989. "

He's a super guy. At the Bike, he asked how much I needed to play the side games during the three days that we were there. 'Well, I guess about $10,000 would be plenty,' I said. 'I'm giving you $30,000,' he answered. He wanted me to have plenty of money to play with in those ring games so I wouldn't be playing scared money. I've been lucky for him in side games and in tournaments.

We've made a lot of money together."

T.J.'s play at the World Series of Poker is always open to Lyle as a backer. "Lyle doesn't get to many tournaments anymore, but he always makes it to the WSOP. As high as you've ever heard of in a poker game, Lyle plays it. He plays in that high game at the WSOP with Doyle and Chip and the Greek and the others. And when they play high, Lyle's as good a player as anyone alive. He's one of the two or three people that play in that game who can really afford it. But that's not it: He's a great card player, a brilliant poker player. He has no fear whatsoever, no matter how much you bet at him.

"In fact, in the final game that he and Bob Stupak played before the Stratosphere thing, Stupak brought it in for $25,000. They were playing no-limit deuce-to-seven with no cap. Usually, they played with a $75,000 cap, which means that you can't lose more than $75,000 on one hand, but that night they were playing the game with no cap. Lyle called the bet with 2-3-5-7, drawing at the deuce-to-seven wheel. He drew one card while Stupak stood pat. When all the shouting was over, Stupak had bet $390,000 on his hand, an 8-5 pat, which is a great hand in deuce-to-seven. But Lyle caught a six and made a seven on Stupak to win the pot. From what I understand, Stupak still owes Lyle some of that money."

T.J. has four World Series titles, along with a lot of place wins at the WSOP. In fact, he was the first man to earn $1 million at the Series without winning the big one. When I asked which year he won the limit Omaha title, he said "I'd have to go look at my bracelet. I've won forty-three titles and I can't keep them all straight. The only major tournament where I haven't won the big title so far is the World Series, but I came in second to Bill Smith and placed fifth to Chan the year that he beat Erik Seidel for the championship."

In 1994, T.J. won two WSOP tournaments during its silver anniversary, one in pot-limit hold'em and the other in Omaha high-low split.

His biggest tournament disappointment came in 2000 when he placed second to Chris Ferguson in the championship event at the WSOP. After starting the final table in last chip position, T.J. inched his way up the chip ladder and finally drew even with Ferguson, the overwhelming chip leader at the start of the day. On the last hand of the tournament, T.J. raised all in with an A-Q and Ferguson called with an A-9. Ferguson won the title when he rivered a nine.

"In no-limit hold'em, you'll recognize the faces at the final table more than in any other tournament because it's the Cadillac of poker. I won the last $5,000 tournament held at the Stardust, the Stairway to the Stars. That was the year that I won the last Diamond Jim Brady tournament at the Bicycle Club, and I told them before it started, 'I won the last one at the Stairway to the Stars, I won the last one at the Union Plaza, I won the last one at the Frontier—this place might blow up next week if I win the big one here, too.' I wound up winning the Bike's Diamond Jim Brady tournament three years in a row. That was sort of a peak for me that I don't think can ever be repeated.

"The first year that I won the Diamond Jim Brady, Mansour Matloubi and I started head-up play with about even chips. I had played with him for about five hours that day at the final table and he never ran a bluff on anybody one time, not once. He wanted to get down to the final two. When we got head-up, he bet me $120,000 on the final hand, and I called him with third pair in a New York split second because I knew that I had the best hand. I'd been chipping away at him so bad that he decided to try to run a big bluff on me. And that was the end of it.

"Then when Tuna Lund and I got head-up the next year at the Diamond Jim Brady, Tuna had $360,000 and I had $120,000. I chipped away at him and chipped away at him and chipped away at him. Finally, he made a $50,000 bet on the end on one hand and I called him with a pair of nines. He said, 'You got me.' And I answered, 'Wait a minute. Before you show your hand, I'll bet you have a Q-10 offsuit.' He turned it over and sure enough, that's what he had. That was the key hand.

"The third year I won the Diamond Jim Brady, it got down to Bobby Hoff and me, so I played a formidable player every year. But in this one, I had three-to-one chips on Hoff, not like the second year that I played when I came into the second day of the tournament with the low chips. The key hand that year was when I had two nines against Hal Kant's two eights, which doubled me up from $9,000 to $18,000 and then I just went from there."

While T.J. is competing in a tournament, he sometimes plays cash games, although there are times when he doesn't play any side action at all. He also occasionally plays in the satellites. "At the Hall of Fame, I had a run one year when I played in six super satellites and got a seat in four of them, and I played in six one-table satellites and won four of those. So, I won close to $35,000 on the side in the satellites."

He loves playing satellites for big events. One year, Berman told him to play in every $10,000 one-table satellite for the WSOP that he could enter, because at that time T. J.'s record was one win for every three satellites he played.

"You get some pretty weak fields in satellites, although at the big one they're not usually as weak as they are for some of the other tournaments. In a $10,000 satellite, you get $2,000 in chips so you can play the game. But you have only $200 or $300 in chips in the super satellites, so everybody's just moving in all the time and you'll get drawn out on a lot. If you only have that many chips, all of them are in jeopardy the first round that you play. Or you'll try to draw out on somebody else, whereas you wouldn't try to do that with a big stack. One year, I played in a $10,000 satellite at the Golden Nugget and five people moved in all of their chips on the first hand. So one guy ended up with $10,000 in chips after the first hand."

Some people advise limit hold'em players to play satellites if they want to learn how to play no-limit or pot-limit hold'em. T.J. disagrees with that approach. "I think that you have to play in a live game to learn how to play those games well, but you can get a feel for how the rise in limits affects things from playing in satellites."

The thing that has made T.J. so successful at no-limit and pot-limit hold'em is his observation powers. "I know what Joe Blow is going to do in this situation and in that situation. That's what helps me. When I'm in a tournament with all strangers, after fifteen or twenty minutes I'm going to know how they play. Say what you want, but there are people who have that ability, and there are people who don't have it. You're either born with it or you aren't. I have a knack for picking up people's tells and all the little things that they do. Caro has a book on tells, but I have my own book."

What about the young new breed of "scientific" players, I wondered.

"There are several good players among the young bucks. Phil Hellmuth is still young and he's a great player. Howard Lederer is another one. Huck Seed's a great young player, too. He took on the best and beat them. A lot of the old timers say, 'Well, they haven't been broke, yet. Let's see what kind of players they are when they get broke.' You see, all the top players have had big money and have been broke and have come back and been broke and then come back again. They're the top players, and that's the nature of the game. But when you factor in how much money you have to make to meet your nut, you have to be pretty successful to just stay alive every year."

So, are these new players playing something like "formula" poker?

"The guys I've mentioned are all very good young players. But all the rest of the new players seem to be the same type—they've read some books, and they all play the same way. I don't think that's good, because I like to see them when they have a few moves to them, a little creativity, some moxie. But you just don't see that among them. The old-type players like Doyle and James "Goodie" Roy and Buck Buchanan (who's dead now), and maybe even guys like me, are dying out. Everybody today is book-learned, but in the old days it was experience-play, where you had to learn your players. I played with a kid down in L. A. who can't win a hand unless money is given to him. But I've never seen him lose because somebody will get in the game and just give his money to him. Any top player would see that this kid doesn't play a hand unless it's a huge, huge hand, so why would you even get involved with this man? Those types of players can't beat me out of any money unless I do it to myself."

Are these new, young players making formula plays and relying on what they learn from books because they don't have the training ground available to them that the vintage players, the road gamblers, had?

"We used to 'fade the white line,' the white line of the highway going from game to game. You don't have to do that anymore because of all the cardrooms and casinos. In California, the new players learn limit poker and most of them don't have a chance in no-limit. They learn to play hands in limit hold'em like second pair and draws, and you can get eaten alive in no-limit with that kind of play. Plus, they only have one move when they play no-limit: They're afraid to play out a hand. So, when they play no-limit, they just put in their whole stack in situations where an experienced player might make just a decent little raise and get more money out of a person.

"You see, the whole idea in poker is to maximize the money that you can get out of a hand. But these new guys are ramming and jamming when they get a big hand, playing limit style. They're so afraid of the draw outs that they're used to getting in limit that they just put in all their chips and put somebody to the test on every hand. But that's not the way to do it, because people just throw their hands away. Say that you have $10,000 in front of you. You have two queens and some guy bet $10,000 before the flop. He might have aces or kings or A-K. You're going to throw your queens away. Why take the chance? Just throw the hand away and wait to pick up another hand. These types of inexperienced bettors aren't going to get paid on their good hands."

These are the types of things that road gamblers have learned; they aren't things that you pick up from reading books at home. "I can remember one time in the World Series when I had two kings twice during the first two hours of the $10,000 championship tournament. Both times, I made a little raise and was reraised, and I threw the kings away before the flop. And both times, I was right: Mike Allen showed me aces on both hands. I knew the player and so I knew the kings weren't any good. It's very hard to lay down two kings; it's easier to play queens because you can get away from them easier than you can two kings.

"But then, I remember a time when I blew it at the Hall of Fame. There was one guy at the table that I didn't know. It was the first hand that was dealt and I was in the big blind with the K-9 of diamonds in an unraised pot. The flop came 7-2-3 of diamonds. This guy led off and bet from the number one seat, the fellow on the button called, and I raised right there. The guy in the one-seat moved all in, and the man on the button (who had turned a set) called. Ordinarily, I would have thrown away my hand. The only player that I didn't know was the guy who moved all in, and he had the A-J of diamonds in his hand. So, I went broke on the hand and went out first in that tournament."

I wondered: Do beats like that cause players to steam? "No, I never steam. I might steam on the inside, but I never let other players see it. But I remember one time when Phil Hellmuth got knocked out of the Diamond Jim Brady tournament. A velvet rope was connected to two poles at each door so that people couldn't wander into the room. Phil went on a dead sprint and tried to leap over that rope, caught his foot on it, and went tumbling out into the room.

"Another time during a limit hold'em tournament at the Diamond Jim Brady, the whole room was completely packed, and you know how much noise there is in a tournament room like that. A Mulatto girl came into the room wearing a dress with cross hatches down the back of it cut all the way down, real low. She was an absolutely beautiful woman. She walked over to talk with Jerry Buss, and the whole room went silent, totally silent. When she finished talking with Jerry, the entire room started clapping, right in the middle of the tournament. In contrast, I was in a tournament at the Normandie one time when I saw an older lady pick up her hand to look at it up close, had a heart attack, and keeled over dead. The two tables around her caused some commotion, but the other tables didn't even stop playing, nobody even noticed. But this girl stopped the whole room!"

Do players prepare for tournaments?

"When I'm taking my shower in the morning, I think about a few things, devise a plan. Then my wife, who's with me most of the time, gives me a kiss and says, 'I love you and good luck.' Then she says, 'Now, concentrate and don't do anything foolish. Catch some cards.' It's the same thing each time."

T.J. also plays in tournaments other than no-limit and pot-limit hold'em, including seven-card stud, Omaha, Omaha high-low split and lowball.

"I never used to play stud tournaments, because being from Texas and seeing what things can be done with a deck, I never liked a game where the same person always gets the first card like they do in stud. I've run into enough cheats and mechanics in my lifetime who could win every pot if the right guy was dealing. And, of course, most of the players in a stud tournament play the game every day, so I wouldn't play in one. But we were back in Foxwoods and Phil talked me into playing the $5,000 satellite for the seven-card stud tournament, and I won it. Then I finished fourth in the tournament, and he said, 'Now you've got to play in all the stud tournaments.' So, in the first 12 stud tournaments that I played, I won one, had two seconds, two thirds, and a fourth-place finish."

Today, he no longer feels unkindly toward stud.

"You know that there's nothing going on in stud tournaments like there used to be in some of the ring games. Except for the year that Larry Flynt played in the tournament at Binion's when he tried to buy off the table. He had a big bet with Doyle, something like $1 million-to-$10,000 that Larry couldn't win the tournament. When it got down to three or four tables, Larry tried to buy off some of the players and actually did buy off some of them by getting them to throw off their chips to him. But Jack Binion had gotten wind of it and he had Dewey Tomko watching the table for him from the side. He saw what was going on, and Larry Flynt was never allowed to come back and play in the WSOP. Of course, none of this poker stuff was in the movie about Flynt."

I was curious about how T.J. opened up his repertoire of poker games to include Omaha and Omaha high-low split.

"The first time that I ever played limit Omaha, I won the WSOP title. I had never played limit Omaha, although I had played a lot of pot-limit. But tournaments are tournaments. You use the same process in every game; you work yourself up to the final table. Final table play is the same, no matter what the game is. So, if you have a knack for playing the final table, you have a chance to win. I know a lot of players who can get to the last table, but very few of them know how to play it once they get there." Of the tournaments that T.J. has played over the years, there have been only two or three times when he hasn't placed in the top three in at least one of them. Usually, he scores at least one victory in each tournament. The place finishes that he makes "pays the freight," that is, takes care of his tournament expenses.

Is it difficult to maintain a stable relationship when you play poker professionally?

"My poker playing is my job, and I separate it from my life outside the poker room. I cannot understand people who can play poker three or four days in a row and then can't wait to get right back to it again; they don't have any other life. I used to play steady in Dallas, five days a week, strictly no-limit hold'em against the best players in the world. Players used to come from Vegas and everywhere else to play in that game.

"At least once a week, we had over $100,000 on the table. This game was played every Monday, Wednesday, and Friday; there was another game that was played on Tuesdays and Thursdays. You could play at noon every day, and then again at 7:00 that night. So, I would play until 5:00 each night, go see a movie, and then go play the evening game, unless the first game was so good that I didn't want to leave it. I followed that schedule for years and I never played on the weekends. When poker is your profession, you treat it like a job. But for some players, poker not only is their vocation, it's their avocation as well. You need some balance."

When they are at their home in Dallas, T.J. doesn't like to go out in the evenings. He enjoys golfing at the country club and then meeting his wife for dinner after he leaves the greens. She likes antiquing and taking care of their home.

"Joy is my support. She never sits right by me at a tournament; she sits in the background. She's right there and she knows that I know she's there. I look over and smile at her, or if I've lost a hand, I'll make a little expression that she recognizes. She doesn't know anything about poker, but she knows that if I move all of my chips in and then get the pot back, I've won; but if I don't, I've lost. She does all the book work and takes care of the business end of things."

When he and Joy went on their honeymoon, they spent a few days in New Orleans. While Joy went antiquing, T.J. went to the track and won $5,000 on the horses. From there, they traveled to Tampa where they went to the dog races and won another $3,800.

"After all our expenses were paid, we came home $5,000 ahead," he laughed. In what other profession in the world, I thought, can you go out for an evening's dinner and entertainment, play some poker along the way, and come home with more money than you started with? "Yes," T. J. said, "but in what other profession can you work all day long and come home losing for the day?!"

Considering that he is one of the most feared players on the tournament circuit today, T.J. actually comes across as being quite modest about his accomplishments.

"I wouldn't say that I'm modest, but I'm not the type

to go around saying, 'I'm the Louisiana Man.' I feel in my own bones that I can play with anyone, and I don't fear anybody alive." That feeling of confidence without the drawback of ego involvement may be the combination that gives T.J. his edge at the poker table.

Like so many poker players and tournament winners that I have interviewed, T.J. admits that he doesn't have that same edge in every gambling game that he plays. Even the best have a few leaks in their gaming activities.

"I've had a lot of holes that I'm trying to patch up. I love craps and over the years, I've lost a lot of money at it. I used to love to run to the crap table all the time and, of course, that hurts your side play because it's so much faster than the poker. But now if I play craps, I don't go to the table with more than $400, no ATM card, nothing like that. I've made several scores of over $50,000 off of $500, but if I go to the table with $20,000 I don't win a single bet!"

It's just another of the lessons that T.J. has learned throughout his career. The rest of them, he has down pat.

♠

10

FINAL ADVICE

In ancient times, the saying was "All roads lead to Rome." In the world of tournament poker, all roads lead to the World Series of Poker.

Winning a bracelet at the Series is the goal of every serious tournament player, I can tell you that for sure. After you've won your first bracelet, you want to win one for your other wrist. And then you want to feel the high again, so you aim for winning another one. The good news is that every year, you get another chance to compete against the best poker players in the world at the most prestigious tournament in all of poker.

And when you come out on top, you feel like a million dollars, whether you win that much or not. You see, it's not just the money, it's the winning that counts the most.

I've been on the road playing poker for four decades. In the old days I played in a lot of smoky backrooms, driving across the dusty back roads of Texas and the South to make my living at poker. These days I'm still on the road, but it's a lot easier now. I can fly to the East coast for a big tournament, get back home for a few weeks, and then fly to Vegas or Mississippi or Aruba for the next one.

And I'll tell another thing that makes it easier these

days. You don't have to learn to play poker by the seat of your pants like we did in the old days. You can learn it by studying books and practicing in little tournaments in a clean and safe casinos and online cardrooms. And boy, does that save time and money!

Tom and I wrote this book to save you from a lot of the work we had to do just to get up to speed on the game. We hope that with our help, you'll be able to shift your game into high gear so we can shake hands in the winners' circle at the end of the tournament road, the World Series of Poker.

GREAT CARDOZA POKER BOOKS

ADD THESE TO YOUR LIBRARY - ORDER NOW!

WINNER'S GUIDE TO TEXAS HOLD' EM POKER *by Ken Warren* - The most comprehensive book on beating hold 'em shows serious players how to play every hand from every position with every type of flop. Learn the 14 categories of starting hands, the 10 most common Hold'em tells, how to evaluate a game for profit, value of deception, art of bluffing, 8 secrets to winning, starting hand categories, position, more! Bonus: Includes detailed analysis of the top 40 hands and the most complete chapter on hold'em odds in print. Over 50,000 copies in print. 224 pages, 5 1/2 x 8 1/2, paperback, $14.95.

KEN WARREN TEACHES TEXAS HOLD 'EM *by Ken Warren* - This is a step-by-step comprehensive manual for making money at hold 'em poker. 42 powerful chapters teach you one lesson at a time. Great practical advice and concepts with examples from actual games and how to apply them to your own play. Lessons include: Starting Cards, Playing Position, Raising, Check-raising, Tells, Game/Seat Selection, Dominated Hands, Odds, much more. This book is already a huge fan favorite and best-seller! 416 pgs. $26.95

WINNER'S GUIDE TO OMAHA POKER *by Ken Warren* - In a concise and easy-to-understand style, Warren shows beginning and intermediate Omaha players how to win from the first time they play. You'll learn the rules, betting and blind structure, why to play Omaha, the advantages of Omaha over Texas Hold'em, glossary, reading the board, basic strategies, Omaha high, Omaha hi-low split 8/better, how to play draws and made hands, evaluation of starting hands, counting outs, computing pot odds, the unique characteristics of split-pot games, the best and worst Omaha hands, how to play before the flop, how to play on the flop, how to play on the turn and river and much more. 224 pgs. $19.95

POKER WISDOM OF A CHAMPION *by Doyle Brunson* - Learn what it takes to be a great poker player by climbing inside the mind of poker's most famous champion. Fascinating anecdotes and adventures from Doyle's early career playing poker in roadhouses and with other great champions are interspersed with lessons one can learn from the champion who has made more money at poker than anyone else in the history of the game. Readers learn what makes a great player tick, how he approaches the game, and receive candid, powerful advice from the legend himself. The Mad Genius of poker, Mike Caro, says, "Brunson is the greatest poker player who ever lived . This book shows why." 192 pgs. $14.95.

BOBBY BALDWIN'S WINNING POKER SECRETS *by Mike Caro with Bobby Baldwin.* New edition—now back in print! This is the fascinating account of 1978 World Champion Bobby Baldwin's early career playing poker in roadhouses and against other poker legends and his meteoric rise to the championship. It is interspersed with important lessons on what makes a great player tick and how he approaches the game. Baldwin and Mike Caro, both of whom are co-authors of the classic Doyle Brunson's Super System, cover the common mistakes average players make at seven poker variations and the dynamic winning concepts they must employ to win. Endorsed by poker legends and superstars Doyle Brunson and Amarillo Slim. 208 pages, 5 1/2 x 8 1/2, paperback, $14.95.

POKER TOURNAMENT TIPS FROM THE PROS *by Shane Smith* - Essential advice from poker theorists, authors, and tournament winners on the best strategies for winning the big prizes at low-limit re-buy tournaments. Learn the best strategies for each of the four stages of play—opening, middle, late and final—how to avoid 26 potential traps, advice on re-buys, aggressive play, clock-watching, inside moves, top 20 tips for winning tournaments, more. Advice from McEvoy, Caro, Malmuth, Ciaffone, others. 160 pages, 5 1/2 x 8 1/2, $19.95.

HOW TO WIN AT OMAHA HIGH-LOW POKER *by Mike Cappelletti* - Clearly written strategies and powerful advice shows the essential winning strategies for beating the hottest new casino poker game—Omaha high-low poker! This money-making guide includes more than sixty hard-hitting sections on Omaha. Players learn the rules of play, best starting hands, strategies for the flop, turn, and river, how to read the board for both high and low, dangerous draws, and how to beat low-limit tournaments. Includes odds charts, glossary, low-limit tips, strategic ideas. 304 pgs. $19.95.

FROM CARDSMITH'S EXCITING LIBRARY
ADD THESE TO YOUR COLLECTION - ORDER NOW!

NO-LIMIT TEXAS HOLD 'EM: The New Player's Guide to Winning Poker's Biggest Game *by Brad Daugherty & Tom McEvoy.* For experienced limit players who want to play no-limit or rookies who has never played before, two world champions give readers a crash course in how to join the elite ranks of million-dollar, no-limit hold'em tournament winners and cash game players. Readers learn the winning principles and four major skills: how to evaluate the strength of a hand, determine how much to bet, how to understand opponents' play, and how to bluff and when to do it. 74 game scenarios, two unique betting charts for tournament play and sections on essential principles and strategies, show you how to get to the winners' circle. Special section on beating online tournaments. 288 pages, $24.95.

COWBOYS, GAMBLERS & HUSTLERS: The True Adventures of a Rodeo Champion & Poker Legend by *Byron "Cowboy" Wolford.* Ride along with the road gamblers as they fade the white line from Dallas to Shreveport to Houston in the 1960s in search of a score. Feel the fear and frustration of being hijacked, getting arrested for playing poker, and having to outwit card sharps and scam artists. Wolford survived it all to win a WSOP gold bracelet playing with poker greats Amarillo Slim Preston, Johnny Moss and Bobby Baldwin (and 30 rodeo belt buckles). Read fascinating yarns about life on the rough and tumble, and colorful adventures as a road gambler and hustler gambling in smoky backrooms with legends Titanic Thompson, Jack Straus, Doyle Brunson and get a look at vintage Las Vegas when Cowboy's friend, Benny Binion ruled Glitter Gulch. Read about the most famous bluff in WSOP history. Endorsed by Jack Binion, Doyle Brunson & Bobby Baldwin, who says, *Cowboy is probably the best gambling story teller in the world.* 304 pages, $19.95.

SECRETS OF WINNING POKER by *Tex Sheahan.* This is a compilation of Sheahan's best articles from 15 years of writing for the major gaming magazines as his legacy to poker players. Sheahan gives you sound advice on winning poker strategies for hold'em and 7-card stud. Chapters on tournament play, psychology, personality profiles and some very funny stories from the greenfelt jungle. "Some of the best advice you'll ever read on how to win at poker" -- Doyle Brunson. 200 pages, paperback. Originally $19.95, now only $14.95.

OMAHA HI-LO: Play to Win with the Odds by *Bill Boston.* Selecting the right hands to play is the most important decision you'll make in Omaha high-low poker. In this book you'll find the odds for every hand dealt in Omaha high-low—the chances that the hand has of winning the high end of the pot, the low end of it, and how often it is expected to scoop the whole pot. The results are based on 10,000 simulations for each one of the possible 5,211 Omaha high-low hands. Boston has organized the data into an easy-to-use format and added insights learned from years of experience. Learn the 5,211 Omaha high-low hands, the 49 best hands and their odds, the 49 worst hands, trap hands to avoid, and 30 Ace-less hands you can play for profit. A great tool for Omaha players! 156 pages, $19.95.

OMAHA HI-LO POKER (8 OR BETTER): How to win at the lower limits *by Shane Smith.* Since its first printing in 1991, this has become the classic in the field for low-limit players. Readers have lauded the author's clear and concise writing style. Smith shows you how to put players on hands, read the board for high and low, avoid dangerous draws, and use winning betting strategies. Chapters include starting hands, the flop, the turn, the river, and tournament strategy. Illustrated with pictorials of sample hands, an odds chart, and a starting hands chart. Lou Krieger, author of *Poker for Dummies,* says, *Shane Smith's book is terrific! If you're new to Omaha high-low split or if you're a low-limit player who wants to improve your game, you ought to have this book in your poker library. Complex concepts are presented in an easy-to-understand format. It's a gem!* 82 pages, spiralbound. $17.95.

THE WACKY SIDE OF POKER *by Ralph E. Wheeler.* Take a walk on the wacky side with 88 humorous poker cartoons! Also includes 220 wise and witty poker quotes. Lighten up from all the heavy reading and preparation of the games wit a quick walk through this fun book. Perfect for holiday gifting. 176 pages filled with wit and wisdom will bring a smile to your face. At less than a ten-spot, you can't go wrong! 176 pages, $9.95.

THE CHAMPIONSHIP SERIES
POWERFUL BOOKS YOU **MUST** HAVE

CHAMPIONSHIP TOURNAMENT POKER *by Tom McEvoy*. New Cardoza Edition! Rated by pros as best book on tournaments ever written and enthusiastically endorsed by more than 5 world champions, this is the definitive guide to winning tournaments and a *must* for every player's library. McEvoy lets you in on the secrets he has used to win millions of dollars in tournaments and the insights he has learned competing against the best players in the world. Packed solid with winning strategies for all 11 games in the *World Series of Poker*, with extensive discussions of 7-card stud, limit hold'em, pot and no-limit hold'em, Omaha high-low, re-buy, half-half tournaments, satellites, strategies for each stage of tournaments. Tons of essential concepts and specific strategies jam-pack the book. Phil Hellmuth, 1989 WSOP champion says, *[this] is the world's most definitive guide to winning poker tournaments*. 416 pages, paperback, $29.95.

CHAMPIONSHIP TABLE (at the World Series of Poker) *by Dana Smith, Ralph Wheeler, and Tom McEvoy*. New Cardoza Edition! From 1970 when the champion was presented a silver cup, to the present when the champion was awarded more than $2 million, Championship Table celebrates three decades of poker greats who have competed to win poker's most coveted title. This book gives you the names and photographs of all the players who made the final table, pictures the last hand the champion played against the runner-up, how they played their cards, and how much they won. There is also features fascinating interviews and conversations with the champions and runners-up and interesting highlights from each Series. This is a fascinating and invaluable resource book for WSOP and gaming buffs. In some cases the champion himself wrote "how it happened," as did two-time champion Doyle Brunson when Stu Ungar caught a wheel in 1980 on the turn to deprive "Texas Dolly" of his third title. Includes tons of vintage photographs. 208 pages, paperback, $19.95.

CHAMPIONSHIP SATELLITE STRATEGY *by Brad Dougherty & Tom McEvoy*. In 2002 and 2003 satellite players won their way into the $10,000 WSOP buy-in and emerged as champions, winning more than $2 million each. You can too! You'll learn specific, proven strategies for winning almost any satellite. Learn the 10 ways to win a seat at the WSOP and other big tournaments, how to win limit hold'em and no-limit hold'em satellites, one-table satellites for big tournaments, and online satellites, plus how to play the final table of super satellites. McEvoy and Daugherty sincerely believe that if you practice these strategies, you can win your way into any tournament for a fraction of the buy-in. You'll learn how much to bet, how hard to pressure opponents, how to tell when an opponent is bluffing, how to play deceptively, and how to use your chips as weapons of destruction. Includes a special chapter on no-limit hold'em satellites! 256 pages. illustrated hands, photos, glossary. $24.95.

CHAMPIONSHIP PRACTICE HANDS *by T. J. Cloutier & Tom McEvoy*. Two tournament legends show you how to become a winning tournament player. Get inside their heads as they think they way through the correct strategy at 57 limit and no-limit practice hands. Cloutier & McEvoy show you how to use your skill and intuition to play strategic hands for maximum profit in real tournament scenarios and how 45 key hands were played by champions in turnaround situations at the WSOP. By sharing their analysis on how the winners and losers played key hands, you'll gain tremendous insights into how tournament poker is played at the highest levels. Learn how champions think and how they play major hands in strategic tournament situations, Cloutier and McEvoy believe that you will be able to win your share of the profits in today's tournaments -- and join them at the championship table far sooner than you ever imagined. 288 pages, illustrated with card pictures, $29.95

THE CHAMPIONSHIP SERIES
POWERFUL BOOKS YOU **MUST** HAVE

CHAMPIONSHIP HOLD'EM *by T. J. Cloutier & Tom McEvoy.* Hard-hitting hold'em the way it's played *today* in both limit cash games and tournaments. Get killer advice on how to win more money in rammin'-jammin' games, kill-pot, jackpot, shorthanded, and other types of cash games. You'll learn the thinking process before the flop, on the flop, on the turn, and at the river with specific suggestions for what to do when good or bad things happen plus 20 illustrated hands with play-by-play analyses. Specific advice for rocks in tight games, weaklings in loose games, experts in solid games, how hand values change in jackpot games, when you should fold, check, raise, reraise, check-raise, slowplay, bluff, and tournament strategies for small buy-in, big buy-in, rebuy, incremental add-on, satellite and big-field major tournaments. Wow! Easy-to-read and conversational, if you want to become a lifelong winner at limit hold'em, you need this book! 320 Pages, Illustrated, Photos. $39.95

CHAMPIONSHIP NO-LIMIT & POT-LIMIT HOLD'EM *by T. J. Cloutier & Tom McEvoy*
New Cardoza edition! This is the bible of winning pot-limit and no-limit hold'em tournaments, the definitive guide to winning at two of the world's most exciting poker games! Written by eight-time World Champion players T.J. Cloutier (1998 *and* 2002 Player of the Year) and Tom McEvoy (the foremost author on tournament strategy) who have won millions of dollars each playing no-limit and pot-limit hold'em in cash games and major tournaments around the world. You'll get all the answers here —no holds barred—to your most important questions: How do you get inside your opponents' heads and learn how to beat them at their own game? How can you tell how much to bet, raise, and reraise in no-limit hold'em? When can you bluff? How do you set up your opponents in pot-limit hold'em so that you can win a monster pot? What are the best strategies for winning no-limit and pot-limit tournaments, satellites, and supersatellites? Rock-solid and inspired advice from two of the most recognizable figures in poker — advice that you can bank on. If you want to become a future champion, you must have this book. 304 pages, paperback, photos. $29.95

CHAMPIONSHIP OMAHA (Omaha High-Low, Pot-limit Omaha, Limit High Omaha) *by T. J. Cloutier & Tom McEvoy.* Clearly-written strategies and powerful advice from Cloutier and McEvoy who have won four World Series of Poker titles in Omaha tournaments. Powerful advice shows you how to win at low-limit and high-stakes games, how to play against loose and tight opponents, and the differing strategies for rebuy and freezeout tournaments. Learn the best starting hands, when slowplaying a big hand is dangerous, what danglers are and why winners don't play them, why pot-limit Omaha is the only poker game where you sometimes fold the nuts on the flop and are correct in doing so and overall, how can you win a lot of money at Omaha! 230 pages, photos, illustrations, $39.95.

CHAMPIONSHIP STUD (Seven-Card Stud, Stud 8/or Better and Razz) *by Dr. Max Stern, Linda Johnson, and Tom McEvoy.* The authors, who have earned millions of dollars in major tournaments and cash games, eight World Series of Poker bracelets and hundreds of other titles in competition against the best players in the world show you the winning strategies for medium-limit side games as well as poker tournaments and a general tournament strategy that is applicable to any form of poker. Includes give-and-take conversations between the authors to give you more than one point of view on how to play poker. 200 pages, hand pictorials, photos. $29.95.

POWERFUL POKER SIMULATIONS
A MUST FOR SERIOUS PLAYERS WITH A COMPUTER!
IBM compatibles CD ROM Win 95, 98, 2000, NT, ME, XP - Full Color Graphics

Play interactive poker against these **incredible** full color poker simulation programs - they're the absolute **best** method to improve game. *Computer players act like real players.* All games let you set the limits and rake, have fully programmable players, adjustable lineup, stat tracking, and Hand Analyzer for starting hands. MIke Caro, the world's foremost poker theoretician says, *"Amazing...A steal for under $500...get it, it's great."* Includes *free telephone support.* **New Feature!** - "Smart advisor" gives expert advice for *every* play in *every* game!

1. TURBO TEXAS HOLD'EM FOR WINDOWS - $89.95 - Choose which players, how many, 2-10, you want to play, create loose/tight game, control check-raising, bluffing, position, sensitivity to pot odds, more! Also, instant replay, pop-up odds, Professional Advisor, keeps track of play statistics. Free bonus: *Hold'em Hand Analyzer* analyzes all 169 pocket hands in detail, their win rates under any conditions you set. Caro says this *"hold'em software is the most powerful ever created."* Great product!

2. TURBO SEVEN-CARD STUD FOR WINDOWS - $89.95 - *Create any conditions of play*, choose number of players (2-8), bet amounts, fixed or spread limit, bring-in method, tight/loose conditions, position, reaction to board, number of dead cards, stack deck to create special conditions, instant replay. Terrific stat reporting includes analysis of starting cards, 3-D bar charts, graphs. Play interactively, run high speed simulation to test strategies. *Hand Analyzer* analyzes starting hands in detail. Wow!

3. TURBO OMAHA HIGH-LOW SPLIT FOR WINDOWS - $89.95 -Specify any playing conditions; betting limits, number of raises, blind structures, button position, aggressiveness/passiveness of opponents, number of players (2-10), types of hands dealt, blinds, position, board reaction, specify flop, turn, river cards! Choose opponents, use provided point count or create your own. Statistical reporting, instant replay, pop-up odds, high speed simulation to test strategies, amazing Hand Analyzer, much more!

4. TURBO OMAHA HIGH FOR WINDOWS - $89.95 - Same features as above, but tailored for the Omaha High-only game. Caro says program is *"an electrifying research tool...it can clearly be worth thousands of dollars to any serious player.* A must for Omaha High players.

5. TURBO 7 STUD 8 OR BETTER - $89.95 - Brand new with all the features you expect from the Wilson Turbo products: the latest artificial intelligence, instant advice and exact odds, play versus 2-7 opponents, enhanced data charts that can be exported or printed, the ability to fold out of turn and immediately go to the next hand, ability to peek at opponents hand, optional warning mode that warns you if a play disagrees with the advisor, and automatic testing mode that can run up to 50 tests unattended. Challenge tough computer players who vary their styles for a truly great poker game.

6. TOURNAMENT TEXAS HOLD'EM - $59.95

Set-up for tournament practice and play, this realistic simulation pits you against celebrity look-alikes. Tons of options let you control tournament size with 10 to 300 entrants, select limits, ante, rake, blind structures, freezeouts, number of rebuys and competition level of opponents - average, tough, or toughest. Pop-up status report shows how you're doing vs. the competition. Save tournaments in progress to play again later. Additional feature allows you to quickly finish a folded hand and go on to the next.

VIDEOS BY MIKE CARO
THE MAD GENIUS OF POKER

CARO'S PRO POKER TELLS

The long-awaited two-video set is a powerful scientific course on how to use your opponents' gestures, words and body language to read their hands and win all their money. These carefully guarded poker secrets, filmed with 63 poker notables, will revolutionize your game. It reveals when opponents are bluffing, when they aren't, and why. Knowing what your opponent's gestures mean, and protecting them from knowing yours, gives you a huge winning edge. *An absolute must buy!* $59.95.

CARO'S MAJOR POKER SEMINAR

The legendary "Mad Genius" is at it again, giving poker advice in VHS format. This new tape is based on the inaugural class at Mike Caro University of Poker, Gaming and Life strategy. The material given on this tape is based on many fundamentals introduced in Caro's books, papers, and articles and is prepared in such a way that reinforces concepts old and new. Caro's style is easy-going but intense with key concepts stressed and repeated. This tape will improve your play. 60 Minutes. $24.95.

CARO'S POWER POKER SEMINAR

This powerful video shows you how to win big money using the little-known concepts of world champion players. This advice will be worth thousands of dollars to you every year, even more if you're a big money player! After 15 years of refusing to allow his seminars to be filmed, Caro presents entertaining but serious coverage of his long-guarded secrets. Contains the most profitable poker advice ever put on video. 62 Minutes! $39.95.

Order Toll-Free 1-800-577-WINS or use order form on page 302

CARDOZA PUBLISHING ONLINE

For the latest in poker, gambling, chess, backgammon, and games
by the world's top authorities and writers

www.cardozapub.com

To find out about our latest publications and products, to order books and software from third parties, or simply to keep aware of our latest activities in the world or poker, gambling, and other games of chance and skill:

1. Go online: www.cardozapub.com
2. Use E-Mail: cardozapub@aol.com
3. Call toll free: 800-577-WINS (800-577-9467)

BOOKS BY MIKE CARO
THE MAD GENIUS OF POKER

CARO'S BOOK OF TELLS (THE BODY LANGUAGE OF POKER) - Finally! Mike Caro's classic book is now revised and back in print! This long-awaited revision by the Mad Genius of Poker takes a detailed look at the art and science of tells, the physical mannerisms which giveaway a player's hand. Featuring photo illustrations of poker players in action along with Caro's explanations about when players are bluffing and when they're not, these powerful eye-opening ideas can give you the decisive edge at the table! This invaluable book should be in every player's library! 352 pages! $24.95.

CARO'S GUIDE TO DOYLE BRUNSON'S SUPER SYSTEM - Working with World Champion Doyle Brunson, the legendary Mike Caro has created a fresh look to the "Bible" of all poker books, adding new and personal insights that help you understand the original work. Caro breaks 36 concepts into either "Analysis, Commentary, Concept, Mission, Play-By-Play, Psychology, Statistics, Story, or Strategy. Lots of illustrations and winning concepts give even more value to this great work. 86 pages, 8 1/2 x 11, stapled. $19.95.

CARO'S FUNDAMENTAL SECRETS OF WINNING POKER -The world's foremost poker theoretician and strategist presents the essential strategies, concepts, and secret winning plays that comprise the very foundation of winning poker play. Shows how to win more from weak players, equalize stronger players, bluff a bluffer, win big pots, where to sit against weak players, the six factors of strategic table image. Includes selected tips on hold 'em, 7 stud, draw, lowball, tournaments, more. 160 Pages, 5 1/2 x 8 1/2, perfect bound, $12.95.

Call Toll Free (800)577-WINS or Use Coupon Below to Order Books, Videos & Software